MW01488052

Claiming
America

My Career as an
Independent Claims Adjuster

Kenny Phipps

The life of an independent claims adjuster is a unique one. Ultimately, you spend more time with your adjusting family than with your own family. I had to spend at least 250 days away from home each year to make a good living. That's how I came to know Kenny Phipps so well.

I've been an IA (independent adjuster) for 51 years now, so I've seen it all. I wouldn't even venture a guess as to how many days and nights Kenny and I have spent out on the trail together.

As you will see in this book, Kenny has seen it all, done it all, or tried it all. He is truly a renaissance man; from rodeoing to airplanes to adjusting. We have worked, cussed, argued, partied, and watched our kids play at the hotel pool together. I am proud to call Kenny a past business partner and good friend.

This book is a mix of advice and stories. The advice is solid, and the stories are true. It's hard to imagine the situations you find yourself in when you encounter so many different people across our country. Be entertained, as well as educated, when you enjoy this book.

Happy trails to all!
Matt P. Fatheree

Kenny Phipps: humorous, motivational, and inspirational are my "descriptords" for him. Evon probably has other definitions, but that is best left alone. I've known Kenny for over thirty years. We met while I was a staff adjuster for State Farm, and he was an independent adjuster working claims for Farmers. That year, we handled most of the storm claims in Altus, Oklahoma, together. Our working relationship was effective and consistently fair for all parties involved. It was almost as if we worked for the same company at times. In my mind, Kenny's most outstanding quality is his positive attitude, both toward his work and personal life. To me, the most surprising attribute is his ability to write poetry and prose even though he presents himself as a true-life cowboy.

Any time Kenny was around, it caused folks to enjoy their work a little more and work a little harder. As I write this, I cannot think of any negative thoughts I have of Kenny, mainly because of his wonderful can-do attitude and professionalism and just being a good man.

Ron Booth, CPCU

For years now people have been telling Kenny and me we need to write a book about our exploits while working on the road. Well, we finally started the process, and the following pages are the result. When you are a kid, everyone asks you, "What do you want to be when you grow up?" Many answers come forth: policeman, fireman, doctor, airline pilot, and many others. However, the one thing I have never heard is insurance adjuster. Specifically, independent insurance adjuster. This is an occupation that usually finds you, rather than you find it! I have been teaching folks how to adjust claims for over 20 years now, and one thing I tell each one of them is that this business is not for everyone. It takes a special person willing to spend days, weeks and even months away from home. Your pay is never guaranteed because you never know when you will go to work, where you will go to work, or how long you will be working. To be successful, when the phone rings and the call comes, you go! Makes no difference who's first baseball game, birthday party or anniversary you will miss, you go! If you are not that committed then this is not the job for you, and many have found out the hard way this was not the job for them.

Along with the dedication to the business also comes compassion for the people you will be dealing with. Most of them have just had something devastating happen to their most prized possession – their home. They are not always in the best of humor. You will be the deliverer of news, both good and bad. You are working with guidelines set forth between them, and their insurance company, of which you had no part in the decision making.

That set of guidelines is their contract, more commonly referred to as their insurance policy. It is your work Bible. Your people skills will determine how well you are able to settle claims, which determines your success in the business. By the way, there is nothing in an insurance policy that says the customer has to be happy, which is a good thing! But you need to have the skill it takes to tell them "No" in such a way that they will invite you to stay for one of the hamburgers cooking on the grill. You, of course, will decline but do so, knowing you have done your job as well as could be expected.

I once told an NBA coach there was no coverage for the loss he had suffered, and he was more than a little bit hot! I think he thought I was one of his players. He was coaching me on some things! But once he cooled down a bit, he told me he had two tickets at will-call for me for the game that night.

Whether I went or not is another story for later in the book. I did decline the offer though.

Over the years, the business has changed immensely. Technology is changing claims work by leaps and bounds these days. It's out running the insurance companies' ability to deal with it, which keeps them behind the times. When I first started, all I needed was a pen (black ink), a calculator, and a clip board. We did not take photos back then, so no camera, however that was soon to follow. I also remember being told to go buy an answering machine so I wouldn't miss any calls coming into my room (Denver, Hail Storm, July 1984).

I remember the first cell phone (San Jose, Earthquake, January 1989), and the first time we began using computers to write estimates (Pasadena, Earthquake, January 1994).

Now, we have unmanned aerial vehicles, or drones, and satellite photos. Yep, the business is continually changing. The trick is you have to be able to change with it. Spend too much time fighting change and you will find yourself standing alone at the station after the technology train has long since gone by!

This collection of reminiscences will bring out the dynamic of the family we as adjusters have on the road. We call it our road family! When you have been home for an extended period of time, you begin to miss working with certain people. While you are working, they are your family. If you need to go to the hospital, one of them will take you. If you need help on a file or an inspection, they are always there. The one thing I have never had in this business is a lack of help. If you associate with the right people, or company, the help is there. That bond is so strong that we all stay in touch, after years of not working together. When I finally do hang my hat up, that will be the thing I miss the most. Lots of good times, good friends and good memories have been made with my road family. After almost 37 years in the business, I will bring some of those stories here with you. I hope you enjoy them as much as we enjoy telling them!

Glenn Smith

Jenny

To my WIFE's best
FRieNd.

Mine Too !!

Love Ken

Claiming
America

My Career as an
Independent Claims Adjuster

Kenny Phipps

inCahoots LITERARY

Oklahoma City

© Kenny Phipps 2022. All rights reserved.

No part of this book may be reproduced in any form or by any means without permission in writing from the publisher, except for the inclusion of brief quotations in a review.

Published by InCahoots Literary
a division of InCahoots Film Entertainment LLC
6501 Southshore Drive
Oklahoma City, OK 73162

www.incahootsliterary.com
www.incahootsfilmentertainment.com

Book design by Michael Allen of InCahoots Literary

ISBN 978-1-7341937-1-8

www.kennyphippscowboypoet.com

This book is dedicated to my dear friend,
mentor, editor and publisher,
Joyce Foy Spizer.

This book is also dedicated to the folks I have met
along my journey as an independent adjuster. Many
are gone now, but they will always have a special
place in my memories. I've had the honor of working
alongside some of the best in the business from
whom I've learned the secrets to their success. I've
also worked with many of the not-so-best and
studied the reasons behind their failures.

Contents

Introduction

The idea for this book has been rattling around in my mind for several years after living life on the road. I have well over thirty years of experience traveling across the country as an independent claims adjuster. I've made nearly all the mistakes that can be made and have still managed to survive this business after all these years. Included in this book are my stories from the road, which I hope you will find amusing.

I also have advice for rookie adjusters as well as seasoned Independent Adjusters (IAs) I call "Claims Fundamental." You'll read what I told everyone I have trained though the years.

Have fun with my book.

Claiming America

America

My Career as an
Independent Claims Adjuster

Kenny Phipps

Chapter 1 The Beginning – 1979

It was early spring 1979. I was a two-time junior college dropout and ex-rodeo cowboy who had no idea where the future would take me. I had recently quit my job at a tire factory and in my opinion I had wasted two years and forty-nine weeks of my life. The pay was good for an uneducated rodeo cowboy, and the insurance was better; it seemed I was using it often. However, the work was boring and tedious. Combine those with the fact that I was locked inside a giant building for eight hours a day, and you can see why it was making me crazy. I needed the great outdoors and some adventure, so I quit.

My parents owned a small motel with a restaurant in Ardmore, Oklahoma, where the present-day Walmart is located. Several years earlier, an older gentleman named Jim Wright had moved in permanently. He had been a bachelor his entire life. Jim had been an optometrist, Assistant Coach to legendary Oklahoma State basketball coach Henry Iba, held an elected state job for the Department of Agriculture, and served under General George Patton, whom he had absolutely nothing good to say about while they were chasing the Nazi general, Erwin Rommel, across Africa in World War II. Jim was also an independent property claims adjuster.

At the time, I had no idea what that was. All I knew was that he would be gone for months at a time before showing back up at his home, Room Six, at the Corral

Motel and Restaurant. He took my cousin, Ben Fields, on the road with him a couple years before and Ben was making good money doing this independent claim adjuster stuff shortly after. In the spring of 1979 Jim came to me and asked what I was going to do with my life. I told him I didn't know, but I had a beautiful young blonde wife I needed to support so I knew I needed to find something more lucrative than building tires, preferably more interesting, too.

Jim pronounced, "Boy, come with me, and I'll show you how to make money."

So, there I was a twenty-five-year-old country bumpkin being told by this seventy-five-year-old man he would show me how to make money. Not only that, but he was going to pay me to learn how! He needed someone who could climb ladders to perform roof inspections for wind and hail damage. I thought about his offer for about twenty seconds, then, I made one of the best choices in my life and exclaimed, "Sure, why not." Nearly every modern-day adjuster owes Jim Wright a debt of gratitude. He started one of the first true independent adjusting firms, which furnished adjusters to insurance carriers if catastrophe struck, and they needed extra resources.

Jim knew insurance policies as well as anyone I have ever met. This was largely due to the time he spent studying them and the way he reviewed them.

He would be driving to our next storm site while I would read a policy out loud. If there was a comma in a sentence, he'd tell me to read the sentence with the comma first, then again without. By doing so, the interpretation the policy would change completely.

One thing he hated, though, was calling it a "policy." It was a contract! An insurance policy is a contract between an insurance company and a property owner, stating who is responsible for any issue that might arise. People will often say, "That's a grey area," when really it isn't. It's simply a policy interpreted incorrectly. Another term he hated was it was an "An Act of God." God did not cause the damage. It's just part of the dynamics of an ever-changing planet spinning around this boiling sun.

Jim had a bit of a reputation as being an old cantankerous codger who didn't mind telling you what he thought. If he didn't like you, you didn't have to guess. He transferred this trait to me, and it caused my termination more than once over the years. I am not saying I've never made a mistake; I've made them all. If you can think of something done wrong, I've done it. But I've also learned from them.

For example, my advice to anyone who asked me a question was, "If you're going to ask me a question, think of the worst possible answer. If you don't want to know what I really think, then don't ask." I was that guy at a high-profile meeting who would ask the question everyone wanted to know but was afraid to ask, and it didn't always go over well.

Never in my wildest dreams could I have imagined the outcome of my decision to take Jim up on his offer. I have been from coast-to-coast of this great country of ours from the largest cities to towns so small they didn't have a spot on most maps. I've witnessed firsthand the devastation Mother Nature can cause, from Category Five hurricanes to EF-5 tornados and killer earthquakes.

Something I discovered during my time adjusting was for the most part, people are good. I have seen over and over when disaster strikes, people and communities come together for the common good, and that is nice to see.

Undoubtedly, the fondest memories I have of my more than thirty-five-year career are the people I've met. From adjuster co-workers to folks whom I successfully helped put their lives and property back together from whatever event had interrupted their lives. Many are now life-long friends and folks I will never forget.

The Bellamy Brothers have a song called, "Hard Way to Make an Easy Livin'," which is also a pretty accurate account of being an independent adjuster, or IA. When you get the call to go to work, you leave within a few hours, not days. Once, I was driving a Suburban with four of my buddies and we were on our way to Aspermont, Texas, to go quail hunting when I received the call. I pulled over at the next truck stop, gathered up my old duffle bag with all my necessities, and hitch-hiked back to Ardmore. Another time, my parents were taking their entire family and all their employees to Cozumel. Again, the phone rang. I dropped them off at the DFW airport and went to work. When those calls come in, your friends know you left but have no idea where you went or when you'll be back. All they see are the new cars, boats, airplanes, motorcycles, and other toys when they appear. What they don't see are the long, hard hours spent working, the loneliness of being miles away from your family, the high cost of life on the road, or the tax man, who has ended many IA careers.

Gold Buckles

I know a guy named Walt Woodard who has been a Professional Champion Team Roper two times. He also puts on roping clinics across the country. I have been fortunate enough to attend two of his clinics, and he told this story at both of them.

If he sees someone throwing his loop incorrectly, he will correct them by declaring, "John, you're throwing your loop like this when you should throw it like this." He will then throw a loop identical to the messed-up loop John had thrown.

John will say, "That's not how I threw it."

Walt will say, "If I didn't know what you had done wrong, I wouldn't be able to duplicate it."

John, still being in denial and not heeding Walt's instruction, would remark, "That's not the way they taught me."

"Who taught you?" Walt would ask.

John's reply was always, "My uncle, Bob."

Walt would continue his questioning with, "What's Uncle Bob do for a living?"

"He's a mechanic," John would say.

Walt would then ask, "Is he a good mechanic?"

"Of, course he is. He's the best in town," John would answer.

Walt would counter with, "Well, if your pickup breaks down, you need to call Uncle Bob because I don't know diddly about repairing pickups. However, if you want to learn how to rope, you need to find a guy who has one of these," as he'd point to his World Champion Gold Buckle.

"If you find a guy with one of these," again pointing to his buckle, "Watch and learn from him or her because they are qualified to show you how to rope a steer. If you'll pay attention, you just might learn something. Most of the guys who have one of these are happy to give you tips on how to improve your skills."

There are old-timers in the adjusting world who have figurative gold buckles, and they are happy to share some of the tricks of the trade that took years for them to perfect. The best way to learn the business is to ride with one of these seasoned adjusters and spend a few days with them, watching and listening."

Don't tell the person, you'll help them. They have been in the biz for years, working claims solo, and having to stop and answer your questions is distracting and slows them down. Some vendors have mentor programs where you can ride along with an old pro. Just be respectful of his or her time.

Here are a few of the places that come to mind when I'm asked about some of the places I've been.

One of the things I rarely got tired of was seeing new parts of the country and meeting new people. There are far more states that I have worked in than states I have not. I've traveled from coast-to-coast to Canada and to Mexico. I missed my family horribly, and I missed so many precious moments with my children that I can only hope to make it up them by spending more time with my grandchildren.

Here are a few places work took me that became special to me over the years:

Minneapolis, 1979

This was the first storm I worked, and I thought I was rich, so I went to an Eddie Bauer store and bought a $300 goose down sleeping bag. Never again would I be cold while sleeping on the ground or in a thin piece of fabric. It would hopefully keep a bear from making me his midnight snack.

Condon, Oregon

This story is a good one, but it's hidden deeper in this book.

Wichita, Kansas

I was fortunate enough to live five and a half hours south of Wichita, which attracted tornados and monster hailstorms. The houses, for the most part, were modest, and the roofs easy to climb. Some of the biggest tornados ripped apart Wichita and the surrounding towns. One was so ferocious that it left four mobile homes out of 300 units standing in its wake, just between Wichita and Andover.

Another time I knocked on a lady's door and she hugged my neck saying she wanted to show me the house I bought her. Apparently, I had worked a tornado claim that had destroyed her house the previous year. In her mind I had bought her a new home

Chapter 3

Sturgis,
South Dakota

In the early 1980s I was working a large hailstorm in
Denver, Colorado, when Matt Fatheree asked me if I
would run up to Sturgis for a small storm. I would be
doing the company a huge favor. He also said I'd only be
gone two or three days.

I was getting bored in Denver and thought a short road
trip would be nice, plus I'd never been to South Dakota.
The closer I got to Sturgis, the more motorcycles I saw.
They were everywhere, and I mean everywhere. The
agent's office was downtown, and as I was getting closer, I
drove by a teepee along the highway with a plywood sign
leaning on it. It read:

Lovely Lana
Poor Boy Nurse
& Tattoo Artist

I parked about three blocks away and got out of the truck
in my normal attire: short hair, dockers, white shirt, and a
briefcase. I looked like a Drug Enforcement Agency
poster boy. I found the agent's office and told him to
cancel all his appointments because he was going to spend
the day with me, since there wasn't a town map.

"What the heck are all these bikers doing here?" I asked.

He looked at me in disbelief before telling me this was

"Bike Week." Thousands of bikers from all over America swarmed this small, normally quiet, Black Hills town. I was following the agent when he stopped in his tracks as he saw a guy holding a sign that basically said, "Hey, Baby, show us your goods."

With a little encouragement from her growing audience, a girl peeled off her bikini top and shook her assets at the audience. That was one of the more interesting days I had that summer.

Abilene, Texas

Doug Cude and I were working in Abilene, Texas, when we found out the town was going to be celebrating its 150th birthday. There were going to be local bands, food vendors, and things for the kids to do in downtown Abilene. We decided to check it out, so we headed to the party that Saturday night to see everyone was having a good time. There were four streets that connected, as in all Texas towns, in front of the courthouse. A band was on each street. One band, called "Johnny D and the Rocking 88s" blew us away. They were the best local band I'd ever seen. We had a couple of beers before heading back to the motel to work.

There are towns I'd love to visit again and then there are towns I hope I'll never see again. Some of the latter are:

Phoenix, Arizona

Sure, it's a dry heat. My oven is dry, but I don't want to live in it.

Los Angeles, California

Twenty lanes of traffic, and no one's moving.

Seattle, Washington

Seattle is a beautiful city, but you'll either work in the rain or you won't make any money.

Houston, Texas and the Gulf Coast

Everything smells like mold, and the traffic is equal to LA's.

After a tropical storm or bigger, the mosquitos can suck a quart of blood daily.

Next are a few towns I could easily call home:

Billings, Montana

I traveled to Billings three times in my career to work claims. One of those times I had to testify in court. You will find more stories about Billings as you read on.

Nampa, Idaho

Nampa has beautiful weather, world class hunting and fishing, and nice people.

Homestead, Florida

Gateway to the Florida Keys. What else needs said?

Claims 1
Fundamental

Don't Wash Your Underwear

One day, while working a storm in Denver, I saw two legs sticking out from under a car. I knew the car belonged to my old friend Glenn Smith. He was still relatively new to the business, and I asked him what he was doing.

He replied, "The transmission has gone out, and I'm working on it."

Now, whether or not he was capable of repairing it was not the question. He was quite a mechanic.

"You need to take it to a shop and let them fix it," I told him.

"I can't afford to," he disclosed.

"You can't afford not to," I responded. "How much will it cost for you to fix it?" I asked.

"Three or four-hundred dollars," he estimated.

"How many days will it take you, and what would a shop charge you?" I continued.

"Probably three days, and around six hundred," he uttered.

"How much can you make in one day working claims?" I asked.

"Probably five-hundred a day," he said as he started doing the math in his head.

I concluded, "Okay, in three days you can make fifteen-hundred dollars. If they charge you six-hundred, that still makes you nine-hundred in the plus column. Or you can do it yourself for four-hundred, miss three days' work and be nineteen-hundred in the hole."

You can't afford to work on your car or wash your underwear.

Chapter 4

Billings,
Montana – 1991

In June 1991, Pat Wardlaw asked if Doug Cude and I would go to Billings, Montana, for a small hailstorm. He said we would probably get around one-hundred claims each. While that's not very many, it would be worth going up there. Plus, I like Montana.

It was an easy storm to work, as it had only produced soft quarter-sized hail. We were in our second week there and knew we wouldn't be there much longer, so we decided to take the afternoon off and play a round of golf. Around 3 p.m., while we were on the back nine, storm clouds started to build. The sky grew dark with a hint of green, a sure indicator the storm was going to be powerful.

We decided it was time to go in, because even though I'm not afraid of much, I absolutely don't like lightning. I mean I really don't like it. We turned in our golf cart and had just pulled into the covered parking area at our motel when the hail started. And this wasn't small hail either. It was every adjuster's dream, tennis to baseball-sized hail with very little wind.

I called Pat and told him to dispatch at least ten more adjusters because this was going to be a good one. Pat hesitated about the number of additional adjusters I wanted him to activate, but he knew I was greedy and wouldn't ask unless I knew we couldn't handle the volume.

All reports indicated the hail covered the entire city, including Billings Heights, and stretched as far west as the airport. By the time all the claims had been reported, we had worked a little over five- thousand claims.

Billings – 1995

In the spring of 1995, another hailstorm hit Billings. Pat called me again and asked if I wanted to return to Billings to be the team lead. The regional claims manager for the carrier we worked for in 1991 had requested me, which meant I would have to go unless I was working another storm. I happily loaded my car and headed back to the "Big Sky Country."

Upon my arrival in Billings, I soon found out this storm was not going to be anywhere near what the 1991 event was. Damages in town were limited to small pockets of damage with no damage outside the Billings city limits. Each storm is different, and damage is evaluated by the size of the hail, amount of wind, roof age, and other factors. This is not an adjuster's dream, because folks don't understand how they would have no damage while a neighbor or friend a block or two away could have their roof replaced. In these cases, I would tell the customer that hail, like rain, has to start and stop somewhere.

On the outskirts of Billings Heights there was an A-frame house with jumbo cedar shakes, which had been painted green sometime in the past. What I didn't know was that the owner had already been paid to replace the roof after the 1991 event. Being that it had taken place at the beginning of the computer age, record-keeping for that storm had been managed using index cards. That meant you couldn't just enter a few numbers in an electronic database to get policy information; you had to physically dig through paper files. The inefficiency of this system made it difficult to pull prior adjusting records.

I didn't find enough fresh damage to warrant replacing the roof this time. It only had a few sporadically-broken shingles and some chips in the paint. I allowed for a general repair to the roof and a paint job.

Billings – 1999

Around October 1999, I received a call from a gentleman who said he represented the insurance company I had worked for in 1991 and 1995. It seemed the guy with the A-frame house—we'll call him Bozo—was suing both myself and the company for bad faith. He felt that we hadn't paid him what he was owed for his 1995 claim, which was, of course, nonsense. If he managed to win, he'd be in for a fairly large payday. Normally, when an insurance company is found guilty of bad faith, the settlement awarded starts around one-million bucks.

The attorney asked if I remembered the claim, and if I would consider coming to Billings to testify before a judge and jury. I told him I vaguely remembered the details of the claim, but I really didn't care too much about the judge and jury deal.

He faxed me the claim so I could try to remember the details and why I made the choices I did. The claim was simple to me. Bozo wanted payment for an entire new roof in 1995, but he had already been paid to replace it in 1991. He never did, though. He just painted it green in an attempt to hide the previous damage. Had I known he had been paid for the roof in 1991, he wouldn't have received a dime from my 1995 estimate, and I would have asked for receipts for the replacement. Once a roof has been paid to be replaced, it's not insured until it's replaced. Unfortunately, that's not how it turned out and will never understand why the attorney didn't do just that.

Things were going as planned and in a few days I was sitting on the witness stand, and the plaintiff's attorney was doing his best to make me look like an unqualified idiot in the adjustment of the claim. Then he made a terrific mistake, he asked me how much damage to the house was caused by the tornado.

"What tornado?" Was my response.

He jumped on my reply. "I can't believe you call yourself a professional adjuster and didn't know there was a tornado associated with this storm. It was on the state news, local news, and the Weather Channel."

That really pissed me off, and the Farmer's lawyer told me later he could tell by my expression that the guy had really struck a nerve and was terrified about how I would react. I asked him if he knew where I was from?

"You sound like you're from Texas, or somewhere in the south."

"Well sir. When you live in Billings, 95% of America is from the south," I remarked. That line got a few chuckles from the jury.

I continued with " You people crack me up. When the Weather Channel says a tornado was in your county, you think it hit your house. What you folks call a tornado, we call dust devils and let our kids run out and play in them." That drew a little more laughter.

"To satisfy your questions about my qualifications Sir, I live in Oklahoma. Did you happen to hear about the Oklahoma City tornado? I have been working it all year." I then turned to the jury and remarked, "A tornado did not hit this house, and you can take that to the bank. If you have ever been behind a tornado, you don't have to ask."

The lawyer quickly told the judge he had no more questions for me, and the judge asked the Farmer's lawyer if he had any questions. He immediately said, "No." The judge excused me. I received a call a week later from Tom, the company's Senior Adjuster, and he told me they had won the case and the plaintiff was not awarded a dime. He told me the company's lawyer said they wouldn't have won without my testimony.

Claims **2**
Fundamental

Don't Forget Family At Home

As independent adjusters we make many sacrifices to be successful. But never forget your family who also make sacrifices. Do whatever it takes to remember birthdays, anniversaries, and holidays. With the capabilities of cell phones today, there is no reason to miss special days with the folks back home. I call home every day, or at least every other day. I know it's hard to baby talk for thirty minutes or an hour when you have a mountain of paperwork, but as John Weibe once told me, "At the end of the day, it's just another storm."

You're Not in Montana Anymore

While working in Billings in 1995, I was told by native folks that I could drive well above the posted speed limit on the interstate highway and the ticket would only be five dollars. They must have gotten their kicks by tricking strangers into getting a speeding ticket and paying the over-priced fine. I had a handful of claims to work in Miles City, which is roughly three-hundred miles away. It was a bluebird pretty day, so when I was headed back to Billings, I decided to check out this speed limit prank.

I set the cruise control in my new Ford pickup to 80 mph and let her go. About seventy miles from Billings, a Montana State Trooper came along. He was very professional and asked me the standard questions about where I've been, where was I going, and what was my business.

Testing the prank further, I told him several people had informed me that the fine for speeding was five dollars, which surely couldn't be true.

He assured me it was indeed true to which I responded, "And I pay you in cash?"

When I asked him to explain, he told me that our dear friends with OPEC enforced a fuel embargo against the United States back in 1972. Fuel prices went nuts, so our government put in force a nationwide 55 mph speed limit on all interstate highways. If the states didn't lower the speed limit, they would lose their federal tax dollars for highway improvements. So, Montana tricked the feds by saying that exceeding the speed limit was not speeding but was instead wasting energy, the fine for which was one whole Abraham Lincoln.

I asked him how fast I could I go for five bucks, and he said normally 85 mph. I told him to go ahead and pull over about a mile ahead because it would take that much time to get up to 85.

He laughed and asked why I wanted a ticket for 85 mph. I told him that I wouldn't have to buy another beer for five years when I got back to Oklahoma and told my buddies that I was fined five dollars for going 85 in a 55.

He just laughed and pronounced, "Get out of here."

While I was there, I worked a claim for a guy who was having a garage sale, and there was an antique wood/coal-burning cookstove. So, as I was leaving, I went to his house and loaded the stove into my new Ford F-150 pickup. I had a trainee, Kevin Keeton, with me and as crossed the border from Montana to Wyoming, he said to me, "Hey man, we ain't in Montana anymore," as I was still speeding along. I said back, "No worries. There ain't a cop within 50 miles of here."

As soon as those words left my lips, we met him. His brake lights came on as he was turning around, so I just went ahead and pulled over. He pulled up behind me. At my truck window he asked, "Sir, what are you hauling?"

"I'm hauling ass!" I divulged.

Laughing, he said, "No one has ever told me that before.

But yes, you were. Black smoke was coming out of your truck, and I thought you were on fire."

Turned out that smoke he saw was coal dust coming out of the stove in my truck bed. While the trooper and I were talking, Kevin asked, "Sir, is it okay if I get out and go pee? I really need to go, and you screwed up our next scheduled stop. He might not stop again for another 100 miles."

"Is that true?" the officer asked me.

I nodded my head.

He then told me two of his buddies were drinking coffee at a truck stop ahead, and he was going to radio them and tell them to arrest me, if I didn't stop.

"On what charge?" I asked.

"We'll think of something," he laughed.

Dive Computer

There have been so many changes in the business since I worked my first claim in 1979, and I can't begin to list them all. Hail is the bread and butter of the business, while hurricanes and tornados are bonuses.

For years all I had to carry was a clipboard with three carbon copies attached to it. We would visit lumber yards to get prices, which rarely exceeded twenty items. The tools of the trade were a dependable car, a fifty-foot Lufkin tape measure with a golf ball attached to the end of it, a clipboard, starched and pressed Wrangler jeans, and, of course, a ladder at least twelve-foot tall. In the early 1990s, computers entered the scene and it became obvious to many of us that they were here to stay, whether we liked it or not. The old-timers who refused to learn this ever-changing technology were left behind, while most of the folks who embraced it went on to a successful career. I was somewhere in the middle, and although I knew zero about computers, I had the best tutor a guy could have. Her name is Carol (Cookie) Smith, and she's married to my buddy, Glenn.

In 1994, when the Santa Cruz earthquake hit, Farmers Insurance decided to pay us $75.00 per hour instead of a percentage of the loss. I went to Glenn, who was a notch above me in the computer evolution chain and told him we had just received a full-ride scholarship. He asked me want I meant, and I told him they were going to pay us by the hour, and it didn't matter if it took an hour to write up or twenty. The light came on in his head and he agreed; we needed to take advantage of this opportunity.

Enter Cookie. She worked for a large agricultural research foundation and had been using a computer for years. Glenn and I kept the phone lines between Pasadena, California, and Ardmore, Oklahoma, busy asking her questions about how the darn thing operated.

Now, the motel in Pasadena where Glenn and I were staying had a pool, which was just outside my door, and more than once I told Cookie I was going throw my magic box into the pool. She always calmed me down and talked me through my frustration.

Cookie is smart and had the patience of Job. I owe all my success in this new computerized world to her.

Fast forward to 2004 – Ft. Lauderdale, Florida.

I had just bought a fifth-wheel RV and was working Hurricane Wilma, as well as the other seven hurricanes that picked on Florida in 2004 and 2005. The RV park we were in had a marina, and the only vacant site they had was right next to the water. There was only about five feet between the water and my RV.

One day I called Glenn, and when he answered, I said, "Nine."

He asked, "Nine what?"

Again, I just remarked, "Nine."

A little irritated, he asked again, "Nine what, jackass?"
I replied, "Nine times."

Knowing he was starting to get tired of my game I
explained, "A laptop computer will skip nine times
across the water before it sinks."

"You didn't?" he laughed.

"Damn sure did," I replied. "You know I've wanted to do
this for ten years now and it was time to upgrade that
computer anyway. You know, I've always wanted a dive
computer.

Fundamental *Claims* 3

Listen

We all know time is money, but trust me on this one. Let
the customer tell their story. You'll never meet anyone
who is in more of a hurry than me, and I didn't mind
telling anyone that my time was short. It took me years
to realize that listening to the customer for a few
minutes and taking time to answer their questions
reduced incoming customer service calls by at least
75%. By slowing down a little, I saved time.

Chapter 9

Heather, Who?

The life of an independent adjuster is often feast or famine, as there is no way to predict when or where the next natural and sometimes man-made disaster will strike. And contrary to what one would think, events large enough to make the local or national news organizations to sell commercial airtime never generate the volume of claims needed to send independent adjusters running.

However, there are certain events that will stop an adjuster in their tracks; they won't question whether they should load their vehicle and await a phone call. One of those events happened on January 17, 1994, at 4:30:55 a.m. The Northridge earthquake's epicenter was in Reseda, a neighborhood in the north-central San Fernando Valley region of Los Angeles, California. Soon, hundreds of adjusters from all over the United States were headed to what was a modern day California gold rush. As you might have guessed, this Okie was quickly packed and ready to roll. After kissing my wife and hugging the kids, I was on my way.

I met some very interesting people while in the land of fruitcakes and nuts, and some of my favorite stories happened there. This is one of them. One claim in particular was in a very nice neighborhood, and when I arrived at the property, I had a tough time finding a place to park my large F-250, four-wheel drive, truck. I saw a

BMW sports car parked on the street with a very expensive Mercedes parked in the driveway. *Hmm*, I thought to myself. *These folks have some nice rides.*

When I rang the doorbell, a guy in his mid-thirties answered. We exchanged the standard pleasantries and before long I was scoping out the damages to his home. As we walked from room to room, I kept seeing photos of him and the same lady. In some, they were snow skiing at Lake Tahoe, and in others they were at the beach or eating at a fancy restaurant. Finally, I stopped and said, "I'm sorry, but I have to ask. Is that Brooke?"

"Yeah, we used to date," He replied. *Much too casually*, I thought.

Cool! I said under my breath.

As we were taking notes on the damages, two things became clear to me. One – both cars were his, as he was single. Two – he liked expensive things. On nearly every personal item that was damaged, there was a price tag taped to the bottom.

We were getting along quite well when I said, "I'm going to ask you something that has nothing to do with your claim. I'm just being nosey, and you don't have to answer. What do you do for a living?"

He laughed and told me he had an Orange Julius stand.

"Where at?" I quizzed him further.

"Universal Studios," he replied.

I said, "That's cool, but I don't buy it. What else do you have going?"

He half-smirked and said, "I also have a little jewelry shop."

"Where at?" I asked.

"You ever heard of Rodeo Drive?" He grinned.

"Yes, I'd heard of it."

"Down there," He replied casually.

"Oh, Okay," I answered.

About that time, we were walking into another room when he told me his most prized possession was in this room. I looked over and saw a crystal sculpture of what appeared to be flames about four-feet tall. The only problem was that it was now only two feet tall.

"What's it worth?" I asked.

"Well, the artist only made eight of them," he replied.

"That's bad," I admitted.

He continued with, "He's dead."

"That's really bad," I added.

He went on, "If you could find one, I imagine it would cost around fifty-thousand. I only paid twenty-five thousand for it though."

"So, what do you want for it?" I asked.

He replied, "I'd be thrilled if I could get my investment back."

"So, you're happy with twenty-five thousand?" I asked.

"Yes," he said.

"Twenty-five it is," I said as I took photos of the sculpted crystal, which would soon be headed to a landfill instead of its rightful place in a museum.

What a shame! I thought to myself.

As we continued taking photos and notes about the damages, he picked up a single piece of crystal stemware, which of course was now two pieces of stemware.

"Man, I hate to throw this away," he said.

"Why is that?" I asked.

"Heather Locklear and her husband gave me this for Christmas," he stated glumly.

Then, all of a sudden, his expression turned from one of gloom to one that looked like he had struck gold. Now, in 1994, Heather was making the transition from gorgeous model, doing mostly shampoo commercials, to gorgeous television star.

He excitedly said, "She's getting a divorce! I should give her a call."

Jokingly, I responded, "Get me a date with her."

"Do you want one?" He asked.

"Uh, no!" I stammered.

He went on, "Really man, have you seen LA at night?"

"N-no-no!" I stuttered.

"That would be so cool." He continued, "We'll get Heather," and he named some other actress, and "I'll show you LA at night!"

"No way!" I answered.

I thought to myself, Wow, I bet this guy ain't bluffing. He can really make it happen.

He asked, "Why not?"

"Because I'm happily married with kids at home, and I would like it to stay that way," I responded firmly.

"Smart man!" he said. "The women out here would take a guy like you, cut his heart out, and then hand it back to you."

As we walked outside, he saw my truck. Not knowing it was mine, he said, "I wonder whose truck that is."

"That would be mine," I replied.

"Wow!" he almost yelled. "That's a man's truck! Can I look inside?" he asked.

The expression on his face made him look like a kid asking his mother if he could keep a lost puppy he'd just found.

I conveyed, "Sure. Hop in and let's go for a spin." As I walked around to the passenger side he excitedly climbed in with an expression on his face of a kid whose mother just said yes to that puppy.

"You're going to let me drive your truck?" he asked in disbelief.

"Sure, it's just a truck," I chuckled.

"No, it's a man's truck!" he exclaimed.

I gave him the keys, and we cruised through his neighborhood. I could tell by his expression that he was picturing himself driving around a giant imaginary ranch in Montana, inspecting his doggies, or heifers, or steers, or whatever the hell they were.

He decided to call them heifers. He had no idea what the differences were; he just liked the word, "heifers." After ten or fifteen minutes we returned to his house. A new Cadillac was pulling into the driveway and a lady who turned out to be his mother was getting out of it. He ran up to her and told her I was his claims adjuster, and I had driven all the way from Oklahoma in this really cool truck. He was going on about my truck when she put her hand on his wrist, and in her best "mother's here to help voice," gently said, "Well, Honey, just go buy you one."

Now, back to Ms. Locklear.

When I returned to my motel room on Colorado Drive in Pasadena, I quickly picked up the motel phone and called my beautiful wife, Evon.

"Hey, Honey, guess what I did today?" I babbled into the phone.

"What, Sweetheart?" she asked, knowing that coming from me, it could be anything.

"I turned down a date with Heather Locklear today," I announced excitedly.

Thinking I would surely be nominated for "Husband of the Year" for turning down such an opportunity, I was shot down on this epic display of control on my part.

Her reply was, "Who's that?"

"It's not important," I smiled.

Empathize

This might be your hundredth or thousandth claim to work, but it's most likely the customer's first. Again, I realize you have other claims waiting to be inspected, but the one you're working on now is the most important one. Treat it as such. I always say, "Act like this is your grandmother's claim. You'd want her to be treated fairly and respectfully."

The Secret Service and Me

In early September 1992, my good friend and adjusting buddy, Glenn Smith, and I found ourselves working a late season hailstorm in Enid, Oklahoma. We'd been there a week or two when the news said President George H.W. Bush would be coming to town on September 17 to make a campaign speech and present some awards. We both thought that was cool, but we didn't think much else about it.

Around September 10, about six guys checked in to the Holiday Inn where we were staying. In a matter of one or two days, the hotel had been transformed into a presidential command center. There were large cables stapled to the hallway ceiling that branched off into different rooms. On each door, there was a photocopied presidential seal and title of the room: Communication Room, Press Room, and so on. One room's purpose nobody knew, because the seal was missing. Rumor has it that an adjuster lifted it, but I can't divulge any information about that until I find out more about the statute of limitations.

Anyway, there we were with Secret Service guys in the same hotel, and they were cool dudes. They were always friendly when we met them in the hallway and were willing to talk about things if they could. Any time we asked a question they couldn't discuss due to security reasons, they'd politely decline to speak about it.

They told us their little troop was normal for every stop the President made, so we did the math and decided there were around twenty groups running around the country in advance of the President. They said we were very close.

One thing they told us was even though you might hear a story on TV about the President making a surprise visit, there were "no" surprise visits. Those being visited might be surprised, but the Secret Service knows every step the President takes.

One day, I found a toy ray gun which one of my kids had left in my pickup. It made all kinds of sounds when you pulled the trigger. I took it into my room. I heard some of the Secret Service guys walking down the hall. The hotel doors all opened to the hallway and I was hiding behind the door. When they were walking by my room, I pointed my ray gun at them and demanded they give me all their money. They laughed. We chatted for a few minutes, and they went on their way.

Glenn, who was waiting in my room, loudly remarked, "You crazy som-bitch! They're gonna put you in a hole so deep no one will ever find you!"

"Relax," I said. "These guys know more about us than our mothers do. You don't think they haven't check us out yet?"

Glenn agreed that I was right, but asked me not to pull my ray gun out again. At least, not while he was around.

We knew in advance that President Bush was going to give a speech downtown, then go to an undisclosed location to make some award presentations. So, on the day of his arrival, I arranged my inspections to ensure I wouldn't have to go near the downtown area of Enid. No doubt the security there would be tremendous.

I finished my inspections and returned to the hotel around 1:30 p.m. As I pulled into the parking area, I immediately noticed two guys on top of the hotel's main roof. They were wearing battle dress uniforms, or BDUs, and each was carrying a rifle. *Oh crap!* I said to myself. *This is the undisclosed location he is using for the award presentations. This is going to be way cool!*

As was my routine, I took a quick shower, put on gym shorts and a t-shirt, and started in on the necessary paperwork for each inspection I had performed that day. It wasn't long before I noticed some more activity outside my window on the north side of the hotel.

I abandoned my paperwork and went to the large window, where I had placed the two large cargo boxes I carried my office supplies in. I hopped up on the boxes and placed my feet on the opened window sill. One of the two snipers on the roof spotted me and watched me through binoculars which he could probably see all the way to Austin, Texas. I made circles with my thumbs and index fingers, held them like they were binoculars and stared back at him, waving the remaining fingers on my left hand. He lowered his binoculars and had a short conversation with his buddy. After he looked at me once more, he resumed scanning for more serious threats.

I've got to call Ralph, I said to myself. *He'll get a kick out of this.*

So, I put on my telephone headset and called my dear

friend, Ralph Jackson, Lt. Colonel, U.S. Army (retired), a two-tour Vietnam veteran, and true American hero. I was giving him a play-by-play as I was witnessing the events unfold outside. There was a farm house about two-hundred yards north of the hotel, across an open field. People, whom I assumed to be the occupants of the farmhouse, were like me, hoping to get a glance at the most powerful man in the world.

Not far from them, I noticed another guy dressed like the guys on the roof, obviously keeping the folks at the farmhouse from harming the President. When he saw me, he started talking to his camouflaged collar. I told Ralph, and he asked if I could tell who he was talking to. I was scanning the ever-growing crowd of people near the main entrance when I saw him.

I described to Ralph that it was a well-dressed guy wearing a blue suit, white shirt, black tie, and sunglasses. He was staring in my direction and talking to his collar. Ralph said I should expect company soon. Sure enough, about five minutes later I saw an Enid police officer trying to sneak up to me.

"Howdy!" I said. "What's up?"

He replied, "What the hell are you doing?"

"Watching the best circus I've seen since I was a kid." I responded.

Ralph interrupted, "Who are you talking to?"

"City cop." I told Ralph.

"Who are you talking to?" demanded the cop.

I replied, "Ralph Jackson, Lt. Colonel, U.S. Army, retired." The cop told me to get in my room and shut my window. Ralph asked what the cop wanted. I told him he wanted me to get in my room and shut my window. Ralph told me to tell the cop he could kiss my ass, because there were no laws forbidding me from enjoying the fresh fall air.

The cop asked what Ralph told me. When I told him, he just about lost what little bit of professionalism he had left.

"Do you see that guy over there?" he demanded.

"You mean the guy wearing a blue suit, white shirt, black tie, and sunglasses?" I asked.

"Don't forget, he has an Uzi machine gun under his suit jacket!" Ralph interjected.

"Yes, sir. I see him," I said to the officer.

"He wants your ass inside your room with the window closed, NOW!" Shouted the cop.

As I quickly reviewed the cards in my hand, I was reminded of a famous song by Kenny Rogers, "The Gambler." "You got to know when to hold them and when to fold them." I decided to fold.

Mr. Bush came and left. I might have seen the top of his head as he was a tall man, but I'm not sure. Glenn came by my room and said, "Let's eat Mexican food tonight." I told him that sounded good to me. As he was driving out of the motel parking lot, we saw the two snipers that had been on the roof putting their weapons into their car. I told Glenn to stop.

Hey guys," I said. "It had to be hot up on the roof all day. Come and go with us. We're having TexMex, and I'll buy you a beer." One of them took a closer look at me and said, "You're the guy in the window!"

"Yep! That was me," I declared.

He responded, "I thought I was going to have to take you out, but Charlie said you were just the idiot in 115."

"Charlie," I said. "Thanks. I'll buy you two beers!"

Claims Fundamental **5**

Never Lie

If the customer asks you a question and you are not sure what the answer is, tell them. They will respect you more than if you have to call them later to tell them you were wrong. And never lie to your manager, either. We trust you will act professionally and make good decisions, but if you don't, say something. Once that trust is broken it is hard to repair. Do not be afraid to ask your team lead or manager for help. That's why they are there.

Chapter 11

Theodore

Sometimes, when we have a big house where we need assistance, we would ask one of our buddies to come along for help. One day I asked Glenn to ride along with me, as the amount of coverage and the neighborhood this house was in almost guaranteed it would be difficult to access the roof. Even though this was an earthquake claim, many of the more expensive homes had clay tile roofs, which the earthquake had shaken loose.

Sure enough, it turned out to be a big house in a very exclusive neighborhood. The owner's name was Theodore, and he met us at the door. We introduced ourselves, and I explained I would inspect the exterior before moving on to the interior.

"No," he said. "You need to see the inside first." I looked at Glenn, who gave me a questioning look. He knew I had my own routine and did not like to alter it. Again, I told Theodore I would inspect the exterior first before looking at the interior. And again, he demanded we go inside first.

Not wanting to irritate him, I conceded and said, "Okay, we'll follow you."

On the way to the garage, he asked if I knew what a Hummel was.

I decided to play with him a bit. "Yes, I do, it's one of those big four-wheeled things the Army boys drive."

"No, dumbass!" he exclaimed. "That's a Hummer!"

With a hint of sarcasm, I replied, "Oh, you mean one of those tiny statuette things that are really expensive? Yes, I know what they are."

"Do you like them?" he asked.

"I don't own any, but I really have no feelings for them, good or bad."

"Well," he continued, "Doreen loves them. She has a whole box of them, and they're all messed up!"

He wasn't lying. In the middle of the garage was a box of twenty or more broken Hummels.

"What are you going to do about them?" he demanded. I calmly replied, "Sir, if you'll have Doreen make list of them with prices, I'll pay you for them."

"Really?" he asked.

"Really." I replied.

He asked, "But, what are you going to do with them?"

"That's the good news, Theodore. I'm going to let you keep them." I said.

"What the hell am I going to do with them?" He asked.

"Anything you want," I told him.

"So, if I picked one up and smashed it on the floor, it would be alright?" he asked with a glint in his eye.

"Yep," I said dryly
.

He picked one up and smashed it on the floor, causing pieces to go everywhere. Glenn's eyes were wide open, as I'm sure mine were also.

When the Hummel hit the floor, Theodore let out a laugh that sounded much like Vincent Price's in that old B-movie when the village constable drove a stake into Dracula's heart.

Mine and Glenn's eyes were certainly wide at this point. Theodore looked at us like a demon had just been released from his tortured body and asked, "Can I do another one?"

"Sure, Theodore. Do as many as you'd like," I said carefully.

During his rampage on the unarmed Hummels, Theodore told us that his wife, Doreen, was taking this whole earthquake business hard. So hard, in fact, she had to go to Vail to get her composure gathered up. Glenn and I stood there and watched as he broke each one, laughing that devilish laugh.

When he finished killing all of them, he looked at me and said, "I'm going to like you."

Next, we followed him into the kitchen. On the countertop was an orange with a piece of glass embedded in it.

Theodore asked ,"What do you think of that?"

"Looks like an orange with a piece of glass stuck in it." I replied.

"What are you going to do about it?" he asked.

"I'm going to buy you a new orange, and if you'll tell me where the glass came from, I'll pay to replace it also," I said.

"Damn," he said to Glenn, "Is he always this nice?"

Glenn replied. "No, not always. You must have caught him on a good day."

About that time the phone rang. It was Doreen. "Yes Doreen, he's here now," we heard Theodore say into the receiver.

"Yes Doreen, he saw the Hummels," he continued. "Yes Doreen, he said to make a list and he'd pay for them," he said, the glee evident in his voice. "Yes Doreen, he saw the orange. Yes Doreen, he said he'd buy you a new orange. What? You're cold?" he asked. Theodore's voice grew louder as he exclaimed, "Hell, Doreen, you're in Vail, Colorado! There's twenty-feet of snow there. It's supposed to be cold! I'm in LA where I have no electricity and no heat! I'm freezing my ass off!"

"Here, she wants to talk to you," as he handed me the phone.

"Thanks for warming her up for me," I said, reluctantly taking the phone from him. It was one of the shortest phone conversations I've ever had, as I just told her I would give Theodore the information they needed. I finished taking notes on the damages and completed writing an estimate within a couple of weeks. Many times, on the complicated claims, I'd go back out with my estimate and do a second walkthrough to make sure the estimate was accurate.

Theodore and I were doing the second walk-through when he asked me if I'd like to go to the set of the Tonight Show?

"No thanks, it's past my bedtime," I said.

"They tape it at nine," he countered.

Again, I politely refused.

"Hell," he said. "Do you want to be on The Tonight Show or not? You're as funny as Jay Leno, and America needs to know adjusters have a since of humor, too. What night can you go on?"

"Thanks, but I am not going on the Tonight Show," I said. As you probably have figured out by now, Theodore was some kind of executive with NBC and one of the funniest guys I have met in my career.

Claims Fundamental **6**

Take Control

Develop a routine and stick with it. If you let the customer lead you around, you are more likely to miss items. Start with the exterior and then move to the interior. You are the expert, and the customer will pick up in a hurry, if you're not. Don't be arrogant, but take control of the claim.

12 Chapter   Meet Me in Montana

I stated earlier one of the things I loved about being an independent adjuster was the interesting people I met during my career. The following story is about a couple of the more interesting ones.

There are times when people don't know what's happened to them. Such was the case in Salt Lake City, 1987. A hailstorm hit the area, which luckily for Buddy King, Ben Fields and me, claims weren't reported in huge volumes. Instead, they came in at a rate of 40 to 50 per day.

This was perfect for us, because we could work every day for about three months without getting behind. It also meant there was no need to call in more independent adjusters.

But let me start at the beginning.

I was contacted by Pat Wardlaw and then dispatched to Salt Lake City in May of 1987. It took two days of driving to get there. I went to the local branch claims office to pick up the claims they had received to date. After I explained what they could expect from us, and what we expected from them, I asked my contact lady, Susan, "Okay, now where is Marie?"

"What did you say?" asked Susan.

"Where do I find Marie Osmond?" I asked. "I just drove two days from Oklahoma, and I want to meet Marie Osmond."

Susan replied, "You don't just meet Marie. I've lived here all my life, and I've never met her."

"I will," I said.

I had been there for about a month when I found myself in Spanish Fork, a rural suburb of Provo. I stopped at a feed store I'd seen and went in to buy a team-roping rope. I had no place to rope, but I thought it would be neat to practice in the motel parking lot whenever I had time.

Ben and Buddy had found a par three golf course within a mile of the motel, and they were playing golf three to four times a week and were still able to keep up with their workload.

While in the feed store, I asked the manager if there were any arenas in the area, and he told me there was a guy named Jim I should check with. He had a business a few miles away, and in less than an hour Jim had invited me to come to his place so we could rope a few steers.

Jim soon found out that, while not the best heeler, I could ride a horse and wouldn't do anything to mess one up. He had a couple of young horses that needed riding, which belonged to the actor, Wilford Brimley. He also lived just a few houses down from PRCA World Champion, Lewis Fields. I was pretty much in heaven. I found myself going to Jim's place two or three times each week, roping as many steers as I wanted.

I often found myself roping with a guy named Brian who could barely ride a horse. Team roping involves two riders. The header ropes the head of the steer, and then turns the steer ninety degrees to the left. The heeler then rides in and catches the hind feet.

Brian missed more than he caught, so most of the time I was just riding down the arena training the young horse on positioning, turning, and stopping. One evening, while we were turning the steers out and unsaddling the horses, Jim came up to me and said he appreciated me being patient with Brian.

"No problem," I said. "I just enjoy and appreciate you letting me come out."

"Do you know who that guy is?" Jim asked me.

"No, I guess not," I replied.

Jim said, "He played football or basketball."

"Still don't know him," was my reply.

"Maybe you know his wife." Jim mused.

"Who's his wife?" I asked.

Jim replied, "Marie Osmond."

"That guy?" I asked in amazement. "I mean, he's a nice guy and everything, but no way is that guy is Marie Osmond's husband!"

"I'm telling you he is. A few weeks ago, when we were roping, he asked me if he could bring his wife out sometime and let her watch us rope. I said, 'Sure, bring her.'" Jim continued, "A few nights later, a Mercedes pulled up, and Brian got out of the driver's side while Marie got out of the passenger's side. I immediately recognized her and asked Brian what was she doing here. When he said, 'That's my wife.' I almost fell off my horse." Jim said.

"Cool!" I responded.

I have met enough celebrities to know most of them are not what, or who, they appear to be. More times than not, they are a huge disappointment. Soon, Marie and Brian drove up in the jeep that she drove in the music video, "Meet Me in Montana," she made with Dan Seals. When they got out of the jeep, they walked over to the arena. Brian told her I was the guy from Oklahoma he had been telling her about. The practice pen is a relaxed atmosphere, and she and I chatted about a variety of subjects. She was smart, funny, and genuinely nice, not to mention, drop dead gorgeous.

After everyone had enough of roping steers, I retrieved a Polaroid camera and asked Brian to take a couple of pictures, which he was happy to do. When I made my daily trek to the claims office the next day, I walked up to Susan's desk and laid the photos down in front of her. Her eyes got big, and her jaw dropped.

"Where were these taken?" she asked.

"Not important," I laughed. "But I told you I was going to meet her, and I did."

"Yes, you did!" Susan chuckled. She never doubted me, again.

"Although it's quite insane
And it hurts my brain
But it chills me out
And then I can go home"

"Trying to Reason with Hurricane Season"
by JimmyBuffett

13

The Fly

There's a theory that somewhere on the east coast of Africa, a water buffalo swats at a fly on his back. Though he misses the fly, the movement of air turned into a breeze that floated over the eastern Atlantic.

By the time it passed over the Cape Verde islands it turned into a low-pressure mass of air, gaining strength as it passed over the warm water. By the time it passed over the Leeward Islands, NOAA gave it a name. In a few days, it started beating up the islands of the Bahamas which, although they had seen hundreds, were the most vulnerable to the rain and wind. Then it hit the magic number of seventy-five miles per hour, which made it a hurricane.

As the water grew warmer, the hurricane got bigger and stronger, the flies on that water buffalo's back headed directly toward the ultimate target of all – Florida!

My phone would ring, and it would be time to play "Dialing for Dollars." The IA firms would pull out all the tricks they had get you to commit to them. The amateurs would grab the first offer they received, while the old dogs waited patiently as the offers got better and better. In a few days there would come an offer that was almost too good to be true, and I'd take it.

All because of a little fly.

There Are No Large Losses

There are no large losses, just a lot of small ones. Don't let the size of a property intimidate you. It doesn't matter if it's a one-bedroom house or ten condo buildings with 100 units in each. Work each claim one area at a time.

An example: roof, front elevation, right elevation, rear and left. Then interior, foyer, living room, bedroom one, bedroom two and so on. After you have entered all of your scope notes into Xactimate, you may or may not have a large loss.

The largest claim I ever worked was a condominium with 135 units. When I sent it for review, it took three 2-inch binders to hold it all, and it passed the reviewing process the first time through.

Chapter

R.T. Redding III

I stated earlier that one of the things I loved about being an independent adjuster was the interesting people I met during my career. The following story is about a couple of the more interesting ones.

On September 18th, 2003, Hurricane Isabel made landfall near Ocracoke, North Carolina. The center passed west of Emporia and Richmond. It was the fastest one minute wind speed measured, coming in at NE 54 mph with gusts up to 75 mph at Norfolk Naval Air Station; NE 61 mph with gusts up to 74 mph at the South Island. The highest tide was at Sewell's Point at 7.9 feet above sea level, which was a five-foot surge. Significant beach erosion was reported as well.

Numerous trees and power lines were downed over a wide-spread area with over two-million households reporting power outages in Virginia. The damage in Virginia ended up being more than $625 million, and there were over 20 deaths reported. The independent adjusting firm I was working for, AllCat, had a contract with USAA, an insurance carrier only available to active or retired military officers. It also catered to politicians. When Isabel made landfall, they had loosened their requirements and enlisted personnel were also accepted.

One day, I was in a new adjuster's room who had been struggling with the whole adjusting process. At that time, we were still receiving hard copies of our claims. I was going through a pile of open claims I found on the floor when I came across one with the letters "B.G." before the name. I have the deepest respect for our military, but sometimes I struggled with their abbreviations.

I kept repeating *B.G.* in my mind when it hit me, Brigadier General.

Oh crap, I thought to myself. "Hey Steve, have you looked at this one yet?" I asked the rookie adjuster.

He replied, "No, I haven't Kenny."

"Have you contacted him in any way?" I questioned further.

"Nope," He replied.

Relieved, I told him that if he didn't mind, this claim was going with me. Didn't matter whether he did or not, but I figured it was the polite way to word that bit of information. He asked if there was a problem with it, and I told him that USAA had a team of General Adjusters that I would pass this one on to upper management to reassign.

Trout or Catfish?

I was working as a team lead during Hurricane Charlie in the Fort Meyers area, and we were staying in Orlando. A team lead has about ten to fifteen people to supervise, train, and review their files, among other things. Paul Roy and I rented a house in Orlando and had a fairly nice operation. I tried to be as flexible as possible with the newer adjusters as I could, but I did have rules. The main one was that it's fine to call me at 6 a.m., but don't call me after 9 p.m., unless it's an emergency.

One evening I got a call from a mother/son adjusting team who asked if they could come over and ask me a few questions. I agreed, and they arrived about 8:30 p.m. with a pizza and multiple bottles of wine. As the evening progressed, the pizza was gone, and we were well into the wine when the phone rang. It was a new guy who always introduced himself as R.T. Redding III (not his real name).

"What can I do for you, R.T. Redding III?" I asked.

"I have a problem," he said matter-of-factly.

"No, you have three problems R.T. Redding III," I said.

"What do you mean?" he asked.

"Well, first, you have the problem you called me about. Second, you called me after 9 p.m. Third, you called me when I'm drinking wine." I slurred as best as I could."

"I'm sorry," he said. "I'll call you tomorrow."

"Nope," I interjected. "Whatcha got?"

"I have a flat roof," he disclosed.

"Let me guess, it's leaking," I said, yawning loudly.

"Yes sir," he responded.

"Why is it leaking?" I continued.

"It's ponding," he theorized.

The two adjusters spilled their wine when they heard my next question.

"Is it trout ponding or catfish ponding?" I blurted out.

"What is the difference?" he asked meekly.

"Well, R.T. Redding III," I started, "Trout ponding is covered under the policy, while catfish ponding is excluded." After a brief pause, he asked, "Uh, how do you tell the difference?"

"That's easy, R.T. Redding III." I said, my mocking tone becoming more evident. "Because there's no such thing. I'm going to make this easy on you. I'm going to ask you a question and I want a one syllable answer. And to make it even easier, one answer has three letters and the other has two. Was there damage to the roof?"

"No," he answered quietly.

"Then why did you call me?" I questioned.

"I don't know, but I never will again,"

Claims **8**
Fundamental

Don't Bury Yourself

It would be a terrible mistake on my part if I didn't include one of the main items that is sure to catch your team lead's eye as well as the storm manager's. That is do not inspect more claims than you can in turn in for review and payment than you can inspect in a day. Now, before you start throwing rocks at me, I realize this seems to be impossible, but what I mean is after you have been inspecting for a day or two you should be able to rotate your claims so you are closing as many claims as you are inspecting.

If you can't keep up a decent inspected/closed ratio, you may be invited to the storm managers office for an unpleasant meeting where your un-inspected claims will be removed from your custody.

15 Dumpster Diving

One of my dearest friends and a great adjuster, Nathan Andrews, was working with another firm at the time. He told me a friend of his was working with AllCat and asked if I could help him, as he was having a very difficult time.

I called him and asked if he wanted my help. He replied, "No, I am going home, and I threw the files away."

I discovered years ago that if someone told me they'd had enough and were leaving the storm site, it did no good to try and convince them to stay. So, I told him what I'd told countless guys and gals, "Well, drive safe." I told AllCat's owners about him leaving and as expected, they were furious he left without any warning.

We were trying to come up with a plan for how to recover the claims when my phone rang. It was the AWOL adjuster. He told me he was in way over his head and that he should have listened to Nathan's advice and called me for help.

About ten minutes later he called back. He told me that Nathan said I was a good guy and would have been more than happy to help. He apologized for putting me in a bind, and the claims were in a trash can outside his apartment, and they didn't collect the garbage until around ten.

When I told Bart Hutton about this new revelation, he said, "Go." Without hesitation, I grabbed my friend, Kevin Keeton, and off we went. We pulled up to the side of the apartment and there were about twenty trash cans lined up, patiently awaiting the garbage truck. Kevin started at one end, and I started at the other. Kevin yelled at me that he had found them. The lid was still partially on top, and it was overflowing with garbage, so I asked how he knew that was the right can.

He exclaimed, "Look! It's full of pizza boxes and beer bottles," which are the two main food groups of adjusters. We took the carefully-wrapped claims which were in Walmart bags back to the office bags and were amazed at what we found.

Each claim was 98% complete and totally undamaged. Kevin and I spent the rest of the morning completing the claims and billing them under the adjuster's name so he would get paid for the work he had done.

16

Trainers

I had a pretty good team while in Orlando. They were in tune and running well when Hurricane Ivan brought major destruction to the Florida panhandle. Bart Hutton, the president of AllCat Claims, told me to gather my stuff and head that way. I wasn't crazy about going, as Paul and I had a nice camp in Orlando, but I understood and soon headed to Pensacola. As you can imagine, after three hurricanes, the adjuster pool was getting shallow. And if an adjuster was available, you could bet he was not the top of his class. We were taking guys that had been working at Staples the day before. One day, Bart called me and said frantically, "Kenny, go find this guy now and stop him!"

"What's up with him?" I asked.

"This is the first storm he's ever worked!" Bart shouted.

I said, "So what? That's no different than ninety percent of others we have."

"Yeah, but he's already training people," he said through gritted teeth.

"Well, that might be a problem," I laughed.

Bart gave me his phone number, and I called him to get his current location. I told him not to move as I was on my way. I got there just as he and two of his students were setting up a ladder. I told the students to stay there, and the professor and I got on the roof, which was somewhat complicated to diagram.

He said, "Hmmm, this is going to be interesting."

"Would you like some help?" I offered.

"Yeah," he said. "Hold my clipboard."

"I don't hold clipboards," I revealed.

I then gave him a lesson in diagraming and measuring. I also told him to stop his training program until he got a release from Bart or Mark.

This was pretty much how the rest of the storm went until I was reassigned again to Tallahassee for a special assignment. Just a heads-up: when management tells you you're getting a special assignment, you've probably done something bad.

During my stay in Pensacola, I took a claim from an adjuster who had totally screwed up. I was relaying its status to a file reviewer in Tallahassee named Richard, who was being very difficult. It was a Thursday, and I was preparing to relocate to Tallahassee when I received a call from Richard. He demanded I have the file on his desk by tomorrow.

"I'll have it on your desk, Monday," I told him.

After a few additional demands and my subsequent refusals to have the file on his desk by the next day, he asked, "Can you give me a valid reason why you can't have the file here on my desk by Saturday?"

"I sure can," I quickly responded. "I've been reassigned to Tallahassee and have to report there by Monday. I'm personally going to hand the file to you."

His demeanor changed immediately. "You're coming Monday?" he asked sheepishly.

"Yep, and I'm going to make sure you get the file," I said.

"Uh, okay. Looking forward to meeting you. And if the file isn't ready, you can take some more time," he added.

I responded coolly, "Nope, it will be ready. I'm looking forward to meeting you, too."

The next day I found out what my special assignment was. The State Insurance Commissioner, which is called the Chief Financial Officer in Florida, decided that it was taking much too much time to close the storms down. But, after four hurricanes, I don't know what else he expected.

Must be an election year, I thought.

He issued a decree that any claim not closed by January 1, 2015, would be fined $1,000.00. With thousands of claims still open, you can imagine the panic that ran through the insurance carriers. To try and close as many claims as possible, Citizen's Insurance decided to run their reviewing operation twenty-four hours a day, and I was selected to manage the night crew, which I affectionately named The Night Club.

When I arrived at the office I'd be working out of, I met with Bart Hutton and Mark Weakly, two of AllCat's owners. They introduced me to Paul Huschelbush, Citizen's CEO at the time. Paul gave me an overview of what was expected of me and asked if I was up to the task.

"Let's do it," I said.

I made it known to the adjusters I'd be managing that we would be having a meeting at 5 p.m. It would be a meet and greet in the large break room we had available. At the appointed time, Richard, the examiner I'd been having issues with, asked if he could address my group.

I said, "Sure."

Not having a clue what he was going to say, he completely surprised me with his short speech. He addressed the group by saying, "Gentlemen, when you're reviewing these files and talking to adjusters, remember they have been at the property, and you haven't. It's easy to think you have more power than you do. You might want to check your ego at the door, because the adjuster you are berating today may be your boss tomorrow. Is that okay Mr. Phipps?"

Impressed, I responded, "That was great Richard, and there are no hard feelings from my side."

We shook hands and got to work.

Return Phone Calls

Not many things will get you in trouble faster than not returning phone calls or messages. Leave enough time in the evening to return your calls and messages. Again, even if there is only minor damage, this is the most important claim they have. If you hurt a customer's feelings, they're likely to find someone else to finish the job.

If you have a claim that you feel is going to escalate into a problem, call your team lead at once. In this business, no one likes surprises.

The Night Club

Our meeting in the crowded break room had about thirty adjusters in it. They represented four of the major independent adjusting firms, most of which had worked for or knew their adjusters or management. They were evenly split as to their experience level, from seasoned pros to amateurs.

The rookies had that deer-in-the-headlights look as I explained that we would be reviewing claims from 11 p.m. to 6 a.m. We wouldn't have the luxury of calling the adjusters who had already turned the claim in for review and payment.

They also couldn't call the customer or the agent. The older adjusters questioned me on how they could review a file without calling those people. I told them money wasn't a problem. If they were hesitant to approve a claim just because it seemed a bit high, I told them to just pay it because I was more concerned about policy issues.

If a claim violated the policy, it had to be corrected. They needed to email the adjuster and have them rewrite the claim so there were no policy violations, then resubmit it.

I also told them if they had a file and were uncomfortable with the instructions I gave them, they could bring it to me, and I would sign it. I reassured them I would not put them out on a limb and then cut it off behind them, because I've had that happen too many times in my career and hated it.

Our meeting in the crowded break room had about thirty adjusters in it. They represented four of the major independent adjusting firms, most of which had worked for or knew their adjusters or management. They were evenly split as to their experience level, from seasoned pros to amateurs.

Around 6:30 a.m., as we started approving a few files, Paul arrived so I could meet with him. Occasionally, he would pat me on the back and say, "Oh Kenny, this one is bad. Really bad." We would discuss the claim in question, and I would ask what should have been done. He'd think about it for a minute then say, "Just what you did."

One morning, after reviewing a few files with Paul, he asked me what my criteria was for approving claims. I held a file upside down and asked him if he saw any blood dripping out of it.

Confused, he asked, "Blood?"

"Yes, policy issues," I answered.

He said he didn't see any.

"If there are no policy issues, I okay them," I informed him. I continued, "The only way to close claims at three a.m. is to pay them. Because of the mandate by the Chief Financial Officer, it's all but impossible to verify the proper amount that should be paid. That's why I just sign off on them. Without being able to talk to the adjuster, agent or customer, we had little choice but to pay them."

As we were into our second week, I was visiting with Paul, and he asked if I knew why he liked me.

I said, "No."

He answered, "It was because you will make a decision." "Now, don't get me wrong," he said. "It might not be the right one, or the one I would have made, but you will make one, look the me in the eye, and say, 'Yes, I made it.'" He continued, "I can't find anyone who wouldn't try to pass the blame to someone else."

One night around two in the morning, I was walking through the office and discovered a young guy sleeping under his desk. I kicked him and told him to get his ass out from under it. He crawled out and begged me not to fire him, as he really needed this job. "Don't ever let me catch you sleeping here again," I scolded him. "Go take a nap in Paul's office. It has carpet."

Amazed at what he'd just heard, he asked, "Really?"

"Where do you think I go?" I chuckled.

Fundamental *Claims* 10

Review Your Work

Review your work. You can't imagine the number claims returned to the adjuster for dumb mistakes. Take a few moments to review your claim.

Executive Complaint Department

When The Night Club closed on December 31, Paul asked me if I'd like to keep working directly under him chasing down problem claims. I told him I'd love to, as there was nothing more boring than reviewing claims. He took me around the offices introducing me to the file reviewers already in place. As you might guess, this caused a little jealousy with many of the file reviewers. Paul would introduce me and say, "If this guy asks you to do something, pretend it's me. He's working directly under me, so stop what you're doing and assist him." They didn't know me and were, understandably, a little pissed I had so much authority.

You might have noticed I wrote "offices" earlier. That's because, before we closed The Night Club, Paul asked me to find an office that would hold the entire Citizens storm staff. I found two identical two-story office buildings that were side-by-side. The buildings housed offices on top of a parking area.

Whenever Paul had a hot file for a high-profile person or situation, Paul would ask me to take care of it. That meant I was to find out what was holding up the payment or progress and fix it that day. I had the best gig in both buildings because I came and went as I pleased and answered directly to Paul. I worked closely with Frank Fine, the commercial claims manager, and Rita Terry, an old friend of mine who managed the residential claims.

They were in separate buildings, and I was in each building several times a day. I noticed I kept bumping into Tammy Boling, who was officed in Building Two, quite often as I was researching problems.

Finally, I realized we were doing the same job and duplicating our research. I told Paul about her and how we were stepping on each other's toes, and it only made sense to combine our efforts. Luckily, that made sense to him too, so he gave us the green light. I told Tammy to pack her stuff and move to Building One. She was skeptical, but I assured her I had the authority to make the call. Later, I found out that, even though I had permission from Paul, I hadn't discussed it with Rita. This caused a minor riff, which took a day or two to heal.

After Tammy moved in, we drafted Tracy Wilson to help us. We had a good team with Tammy as the main point of contact, since she could sell ice cream to an Eskimo. Tracy was a wiz with research and policy interpretation, and I worked well with the field adjusters and on construction issues.

Tammy came up with the name Executive Complaint Department, and our little group helped close some rather complex and high-profile claims.

Find Damage

It is very important to find damage. Even if you know the damage will not exceed the deductible, you owe it to the customer to find any and all damage. When the customer has a list to give you, politely hand it back to them and tell them you'll compare it after you inspect the property. You'd be surprised how a hail-damaged birdbath can ease their apprehensions about you.

Chillin'

Working claims, especially catastrophic claims, is a high stress business that can stress the calmest person you know to a point of despair you have rarely witnessed. Insurance carriers have deadlines and criteria about how they want their claims handled. Independent adjusting firms have deadlines too, and the fear that their claims will be taken away and reassigned to another IA firm is real.

The adjuster often feels he or she is on a desert island with no friends or anyone to talk to. He is bombarded with questions from his team lead, his assigned desk adjuster, or the file examiner. The adjuster eventually needs to unwind, or they will have a melt-down, which may cause the adjuster to toss their claims in a trash dumpster and abandon the storm site.

The following is a sample of some of the pranks that I've seen, witnessed and occasionally participated in.

Magic Televisions:

There were about ten to twelve adjusters working a fall windstorm in Tulsa, Oklahoma, one year. The motel rooms opened to the outside, and I had my normal paperwork clothes on, which consisted of gym shorts and a t-shirt. My curtains were open, and the television was on just for the noise. I was working on an estimate when the volume started to increase, so I turned it down. Soon, it started to increase again. Thinking it must be a power surge I looked under my desk and unplugged it. While I was under the desk, I noticed movement outside. It turned out to be Gerald Elrod and Glenn Smith. Gerald had the TV remote, and they were hiding outside jacking with my TV.

Their next stop was Buddy and Audrey's room. Glenn was in the room, and he said, "Hey Buddy, did you know these TVs are voice-controlled?"

"What do you mean?" Buddy asked.

"Just watch, and you will be amazed." Glenn said.

Glenn looked at the TV and commanded, "TV, volume up."

As the volume started getting louder, Buddy and Audra's jaws dropped.

Glenn then said, "Channel, up," and of course, it did. Buddy and Audra were sitting there totally blown away by the wonders of technology when they heard giggling outside their room.

Before long the magic televisions had been exposed to just about every room in the motel.

PGA Tournament:

Glenn and I were working a windstorm in California's Bay Area and were staying in a Ramada Inn in Pleasanton, California. We were getting stressed by the California traffic, smog, and other things. We decided to take a Sunday afternoon off and play a round of mini golf at a nearby course.

One trait all successful adjusters have, that they probably deny, is that they all are competitive. We were in the back nine and Glenn was ahead a couple of holes when I found a baby's pacifier. I quietly picked it up, put it in my pocket, and started putting like Tiger Woods although he hadn't been born yet. When the scores were tallied at the end of the game, I found I had won by a couple of holes.

Glenn didn't take losing very well and threw a little fit. I took the pacifier from my pocket, handed it to Glenn, and watched as his little fit turned into a major fit. He was mad at me for a few days after that.

National Hot Rod Association:

One of my adjuster friends, who is retired like me, was in a big time drag racer earlier in his life. His racing name back in the 70s was Kansas John Weibe. His dragster is in the NHRA Hall of Fame in Gainesville, Florida.

Glenn Smith, John, and I were working a storm in Dallas, Texas, examining claims when we found we needed to blow off some steam. We went to a pizza joint and had a couple of beers along with our pizza. After dinner we went to an amusement park that had miniature dragsters. They stayed on their course thanks to a metal rail that ran the length of the track between the wheels of the little dragsters. Glenn and I split the admission fee since we had kind of kidnapped John. He thought there was no way they could simulate the feel of a real dragster, but Glenn and I finally got him in a car, and soon there were six cars total in the race.

I don't know how we did it, but Glenn won the first race, and I won the second, which didn't please John at all. We were celebrating that two Okies had beat the great John Weibe. John stood in front of the Christmas tree, which had two sets of vertical lights for each lane. He proceeded to stare at it for a few more races.

After a while, he said with determination, "Okay, boys, let's try it again."

Glenn and I didn't win another race that night.

Naked and Afraid:

I was working a storm in Denver, Colorado, and had a claim for a lady who was the manager of a large department store. We got along well, and she told me about a few of the crazy things she had experienced in her line of work. I told her a few of the things I had seen and asked her where I could find a mannequin.

"Why would you want one of those?" she asked. I told her my reasoning, and she laughed.

"You are truly wicked," she said.

A few days later I had forgotten our conversation. She called me and told me where I could get a mannequin. I assured her I'd have it back to her in a few days. After being in a motel for a month or two, you get to know the staff pretty well. I told the manager my plan, and she agreed to let me into the room of my victim as long as she accompanied me and for security reasons. I placed the naked mannequin in the shower and shut the curtain. Sure enough, as was his usual habit, Jim soon arrived back to the motel and undressed to take a refreshing shower. He pulled the curtain back, and there they both were, naked and afraid.

Jim told me he nearly had a heart attack until he realized he'd been set up, and I was the most likely culprit. I pled nolo contendere and told him I would buy his dinner in exchange for the entertainment. He did say she was kind of cute, though.

Claims **12**
Fundamental

Be a Pro

You will encounter people in this business from every walk in life. From garbage collectors to the ultra-rich, to celebrities (not disparaging garbage collectors). Act, look, and dress like a professional, and you will get more respect from the customer.

Chapter 20

You Won!

The funniest prank I've ever seen was not one I came up with, but one that my good friend, Nathan Andrews, pulled off.

He was working Hurricane Andrew in Homestead, Florida, and the Powerball lottery was up to a ridiculous payout. I don't remember the name of his buddy, so I'll just call him Bob.

Like most adjusters, he left his door open just a little so other adjusters could come and go without making the occupant of that room get up to open the door.

Nathan had gone to Bob's room on the way to eat. Bob was on the phone, so Nathan was standing around when he saw the lottery tickets laying by the TV. Nathan eased over to take a peek, and sure enough, they were for the upcoming drawing that Saturday night. Nathan quietly wrote down the numbers on one ticket and placed them back on the TV stand.

Saturday night finally arrived, and Nathan walked into Bob's room and asked Bob if he had watched the lottery drawing. Bob said no, as he hadn't had time. "Well, here they are," Nathan said in his slow southern drawl. "I didn't get one damned number."

Bob thanked Nathan for bringing him the winning

number. He turned white and his eyes got big when he saw that one set of numbers matched.

Nathan told us the rest of the night was a blur. Big steaks, lots of booze, possibly a "Gentlemen's" club, and Bob picked up the tab for every bit of it.

I asked Nathan what happened when Bob found out it was a joke.

"Oh," Nathan's words poured out as slow as cold honey. "He was a little pissed off."

"A little?" I gasped. "A little?!"

"I would have killed you," I laughed.

Claims Fundamental 13

Work with Your File Reviewer

After you close your first two or three claims, take them to your team lead for review. Make any revisions without arguing or getting upset. This is not about you vs. them, it's about working together to have a quality finished product that you are proud have your name on.

21

Chapter

Summit Springs – 1995

In early July 1995, I went to Denver, Colorado, for a small storm. Upon arriving, the storm manager, Ed, gave me my assignments and said, "Oh, by the way, we're not paying for any wood roofs here."

"What do you mean, 'We're not paying for any wood roofs?'" I questioned.

Ed replied, "The regional claims manager said the hail from this storm wasn't big enough to damage a good roof, and he's not paying for roofs that are worn out. Period."

"You can't do that Ed," I rebutted. "There's nowhere in the policy that says old roofs aren't covered just because they're old. You can depreciate them based on age and condition, but the depreciated amount is refundable when the roof is replaced."

Ed said, "I'm aware of that, but he's the boss and you need to do as he says, or you may never work Colorado again."

I decided to work my claims and see what I found before saying any more about it. Sure enough, I had about ten claims on worn out wood roofs that needed replacing before the storm had even hit. They were old, thin, cedar shingles that crumbled under my feet as I walked across them.

I wrote two estimates for each one of those claims: one, with recoverable depreciation taken into account, and the other with depreciation not reimbursed at all. Ed looked at both estimates and noted there was no fee bill. When he questioned me about it, I told him the company was operating in bad faith and I didn't want my name anywhere on those claims. This pissed him off a great deal because he made a commission on each claim.

He was right about one thing, though. I never worked Colorado, again.

As the storm was wrapping up, I had run out of clean work clothes. This wasn't a problem, though, since I would be home in a couple of days. I was packing my Ford F-250 four-wheel drive pickup when I got a call from Pat Wardlaw. He informed me he needed Ben and me to go to Oregon to work another small storm. I called Evon and told her I had good news and bad news.

"What the good news?" she asked.

"I'm on I-25," I replied.

She then knowingly asked, "What's the bad news?"

"I'm going north," I answered. "There was a hailstorm in Oregon, and they want Ben and me to take care of it." My beautiful wife understood that I'd never turn down work because we never know when the next storm would hit. She simply asked me to be safe and drive carefully.

As we pulled into Richland, Washington, we saw many vehicles with their windshields broken out and massive dents on their hoods. We stopped at the local agent's office and came up with a plan. Ben would stay in the Kennewick-Richland area and I would go to a small town called Condon, about a hundred miles away.

When I arrived in Condon a few hours later, I received the first shock of many during my stay. I checked into the local eight-room motel—yes, eight rooms—and the gentleman who checked me in, who must have had throat cancer in the past, was using one of those little devices that had to be held up to his throat to speak.

Not wanting to appear insensitive, I quickly told him I would be making many phone calls and asked if it would be a problem. He informed me it would be no problem since none of the motel rooms had phones. My heart quit beating.

Shock Number Two:

Feeling a bit lightheaded and dizzy, I set off to find the agent and somewhere to wash my clothes. I found the agent's office, and after introductions were exchanged, I asked him where the nearest laundromat was. He laughed and asked where I'd come from.

I told him I had driven in from Hermiston, which was roughly about one-hundred miles away. Still laughing, he informed me that was the nearest one.

Shock Number Three:

By this time I was starting to feel nauseous. I told him about the phone situation, and he said that'd be no problem.

He picked up his phone, dialed a number without

looking it up, and said, "Hey Beverly, this is Jay. Say, I need a phone put in," he continued. He put his hand over the phone and asked me, "What room are you in?"

"He's in room four. Thanks, dear," he remarked as he ended the conversation with Beverly and back at me, he said, "You'll have a phone within two hours." Even though this was good news, it was still a shock either way. I entered it in the plus column.

Shock Number Four:

"Now, what else can I do for you?" Jay asked.

I thought for a second and responded, "Do you have a town map?"

His reply was not a shock.

Having no map, I instead gathered up the claims he had on his desk and asked him to pick out four which best represented the four sides of town. That way, I could get an idea of how bad the town was hit.

Later, as I worked through the claims, Jay met me at every house and quizzed me about anything he could think of. He asked what hail damage looks like if a roof was a total loss, and so on.

Shock Number Five:

About the time we arrived at house number three, Jay gave me Shock Number Five. He told me that Gretchen, his wife, said she would feed me and wash my dirty laundry if I would stop by later.

Jay gave me directions to his house. After I had showered and put on my cleanest dirty shirt, I knocked on their door. Gretchen was a funny gal, who could cook with the best of them, and proceeded to give me Shock Number Six.

Shock Number Six:

She loved dark rum and Jimmy Buffett.

After a delicious meal, we knocked down the better part of a fifth of rum and listened to old eight tracks of Jimmy. *I've found heaven*, I thought to myself. The next day found me with a bit of a rum-induced headache, which I've had a few times before, but I went ahead and got started working claims. There were only two insurance agencies in town so naturally, I ran into the adjuster working for the other agency around mid-morning. He was a staff adjuster and more than a little arrogant.

"Finding anything?" he asked.

"Yes, they're all hammered," I replied.

"Well, that's the way you independents make your living totaling everything so you can charge more," he retorted. I asked him where he lived, and found he was from Seattle. Then I asked if he had ever worked a hailstorm of this size before and found, of course, he hadn't.

Chuckling silently, I whispered, "Good luck."

What he didn't know was this storm is any adjuster's dream. The hail had ranged from baseball to softball size and was fairly soft. This meant it fell nearly straight down without much damage to windows, siding and such. Hail like this pretty well guaranteed damage to the membrane of the shingles, while leaving the decking undamaged.

Every morning I had breakfast at a little Tastee Freez type of establishment, where the owner and I became pretty good friends. I also ate at the Elk's Lodge for supper, were I became known as "The Guy from Oklahoma." I was a celebrity.

One evening after supper, I called everyone's attention to make a statement.

"Okay, folks. I'm working as hard as I can to get everyone's house looked at as soon as possible, but the reality is that someone gets to be first and someone has to be last."

I continued, "Since I don't know any of you, I just want to let you know I'm not giving preference to anyone. Thank you."

As I turned back to my table, I saw two fresh rum-and cokes. I'd already had two.

Addressing the room again, I said, "I need to say one more thing. If you nice people don't stop buying me drinks, I'm going to start eating supper in Hermiston. I don't function very well when I'm hungover."

Condon is located in the heart of wheat country, and the harvest was in full gear. My normal routine is to make my inspections early and do my paperwork afterwards. More than once, I'd be sitting in my gym shorts and t-shirt doing my paperwork when there'd be a knock on my motel door. As always, I would answer the door and some gentleman would be standing on the other side asking, "Are you the guy from Oklahoma?" They usually added something like, "I know you're busy, but the harvesters will be here in two days. Could you please come to my place before they come out?" I'd always say yes, but I'd also inform them I wasn't changing back into my Dockers and button-down shirt. To which they'd almost always reply, "I don't care if you come out naked. Thanks for helping me out."

I met one guy who stood out from the others because he had a strange occupation. He was a professional competitive logger and participated in logging competitions, such as log rolling, tree climbing and so on.

What really got my attention was the saw. He had a Harley Davidson Sportster motor on it. Needless to say, he was a hulk – I couldn't even lift it up. I also couldn't image the torque this thing produced.

Okay, on to a little trivia about Condon.

One evening, after enjoying one of Gretchen's dinners, I asked about the name Condon. "I'm sure you've considered the fact that the name Condon is only a letter away from being the uncomfortable contraception aid," I started.

"Yes," Jay said. "I'm very aware of that." He added, "The town was named after a postman who worked delivering mail there for years."

"What was the original name?" I quizzed him.

He responded, "Summit Springs."

"What?!" I said in disbelief. "You took a romantic name like Summit Springs and changed it to Condom... oops, I meant Condon?" I blurted.

"Yes, it sounds crazy, don't it?" Jay responded with a smile.

The morning, as I was getting ready to leave, I was eating breakfast at the Tasty Freez when the owner asked if he could sit and visit.

"Sure, what's on your mind?" I rendered, happy to have one last chat with him.

He said confidently, "I don't know what they're paying you, but it ain't enough."

"It's not bad." I replied.

He continued, "I'm sure it is. I can tell by the way you dress and your pickup. But the town knows everyone would have been screwed if you hadn't come here. The other guy hasn't totaled a single roof."

"I was just doing my job. I didn't pay for anything that wasn't justified." I said.

He thanked me and said, "Well, the people of this town appreciate what you have done. You could have been like him and no one would have been the wiser."

"Well, thank you," I told him. "It's nice that folks appreciate and recognize that I'm here to help."

Pay

The following statement is sure to turn heads because it goes against all logic, unless you know the reasoning behind it.

The person who knows how to do something will always work for the person who knows why to do it that way.

It is not the adjuster's job to save the insurance carrier a dime.

As I mentioned earlier, an insurance policy is a contract and defines what is and isn't covered. The adjuster's job is to write an estimate that covers everything damaged by a covered loss, no more – no less. I can't tell you how many times a customer has said to me, "I guess you get paid by the amount you save the company."

However, nothing is further from the truth. An adjuster is paid based on the total amount of the claim, because in theory, larger claims take more time to work.

Biting the Hand

In 2005 and 2006, I found myself working commercial claims in south Florida, primarily in the Miami and Fort Lauderdale area. A large portion of my claims were condominiums and townhouses.

One claim had 135 structures. When I printed the final report, it took three two-inch binders to hold all the paper. It passed the file examiners' review on the first submission.

Then, there was Bayside Towers (not the real name). I had reached an agreed price with a public adjuster, which is not always easy to do, of $249,000.00.

Meanwhile, the examiner was ripping my report apart. She wanted a picture with caption of every single item that was damaged, even though any adjuster or contractor would know that you may need to replace "A" to repair "B" in many instances. She was relentless, always asking, "Why did you pay for this? Why did you pay for that?" Finally, the examiner wore me down and asked one too many times why I had paid for something. I was tired of all the questions, so I answered, "I don't remember."

She asked, "What don't you remember?"

"I don't remember you being there. If I included something in my estimate, it means there was damage to it, even if I didn't take a photo of it," I retorted. "I think I'll just send a quality control agent down to check you out," she threatened. Growing irritated, I countered, "Well, you just send his happy ass down here."

On the day of our meeting, I was waiting for the quality control agent at the property in question when I saw him drive up. I knew I was in trouble the moment he got out of his car. He looked like one of those evangelical preachers that you immediately change the channel on.

He didn't have a hair on his head out of place—the kind you just want to sneak up behind and ruffle it up—making him look like he was on the tail end of a three-day bender.

We spent a few hours on the property taking notes and inspecting some of the areas of contention. Although our disdain for each other was evident, I thought we both handled the situation rather well.

A couple days later, I was informed the claim had been re-assigned to another adjuster. I called the PA and told him my estimate was no longer valid as it had been re-assigned. He was livid. "We both have a lot of time and energy involved in this claim," he said. "I'm going to stick this claim up their ass," he assured me.

Fast forward to the following fall, where I found myself working for the same company. I was, you guessed it, doing file reviews. I attended a wind conference in Tampa when I bumped into the PA.

"Hey! Whatever came of that claim on Bayside Towers?"

I asked. He smiled and exclaimed, "I told you I was going to stick it up their ass. I settled the claim for $500,000 and change."

"Well, good for you! They deserved it," I laughed.

When I got back to our office, I started wondering about the claim. Since I had access to the information, I decided to see if I could pull it up. Sure enough, there it was. It was a very interesting read, too. My original estimate was used to get $249,000 of the total claim. There were also extensive add-ons that I didn't have a clue where he got the numbers from.

However, the thing that set me off was buried in the three-page report. He wrote that I shouldn't be assigned any more commercial claims without further training. As you can imagine, that got to me. I got on the company directory and there he was. He was even in the same building! So, I took his report and went in search of my old friend. I found him in his little cubical, hair still perfectly coifed.

"Hi. Remember me?" I asked.

"Uh, yes. We met at, uh, hmm," he said, struggling to remember exactly where he knew me from.

"Bayside Towers," I finished for him

"Oh yes! What can I do for you?" he answered, a bit too smugly.

"Well, quite a bit actually," I started. "I had an agreed price with a PA for $249,000.00 and you had it reassigned to someone, maybe yourself, and ended up paying $500,000 plus change."

"Then you went on to say I needed further training," I continued, my voice dripping with sarcasm. "Just where do I find a class where I learn to screw up a closed claim so bad that it ends up being paid double for?"

I added, "Plus, it's obvious you used my estimate to get at least half of it, so I should be paid for my time and expenses. According to the fee schedule, that would be around ten grand."

This conversation took place around 9:30 in the morning. By 11:00 a.m., I was escorted from the building by Jim Oxendine, liaison for the IA firm I was working for and the insurance company. I stopped by a florist on the way to our RV park and gave a beautiful arrangement to Evon when I got back to our RV.

After a few minutes, she realized this was a workday and asked why I was home so early.

"Oh! I got fired," I said casually.

"What the hell are we going to do?" she cried.

Now, our daughter and her Navy husband were stationed just across the Florida-Georgia line in Kings Bay, Georgia, which is where we were at the time.

I looked at my wife and said, "I figured you'd stay here in Kings Bay with Ashley, and I'd go to Key Largo and go fishing with my buddy Rick for a week." But that's a different story.

Claims 15
Fundamental

Start Each Conversation
with "Dear Judge"

Start each conversation with "Dear Judge." When
entering notes into your file, write them as if you are on
trial, because some day you may be defending yourself
before a jury. So, write them as if these twelve people are
going to decide your fate, because they might.

Claims 16
Fundamental

Scoping

When scoping the damages, write them down in the
order you will enter them into the software you are using.
Start with the exterior, then the interior, and proceed
room by room.

There's an old saying, "Just tell a story." When a file
reviewer or desk adjuster reviews your claim, it should
tell the story of the claim. File reviewers are usually older
adjusters who know their business, and they get to know
how good an adjuster is by the quality of their work.

Chapter 23

Big Rock
in Little Rock

There was a time when the insurance company I worked for developed what they called the Large Loss Unit. Whenever they received a large loss, which was usually a fire, they'd turn it over to one of the guys on this insurance SWAT team to handle the claim as soon as possible. We were expected to be on location the next day and it didn't matter how. We could fly, drive, or rent a canoe, if necessary, so long as we got there.

I was at home one day when Pat Wardlaw called to tell me they had a fire in Little Rock.

"Can you go?" he asked.

"Sure," I said.

I threw the necessary tools of the trade in my car and left before daylight the next morning. Upon arrival, I went to the branch claims office (BCO) to get the loss report and other information I might need. Three local adjusters informed me that the house appeared to be totaled and was owned by a young single mom. They also informed me there was no mortgage on the house and she had an endorsement for a $10,000 ring, which they made clear that they were sure it was lost in the fire. Their non-professional attitudes pissed me off, and I left to meet her at the location of loss.

The house was a modest wood-framed structure and was indeed a total loss. There were only three walls still standing. She arrived shortly after with her toddler, and I told her I would authorize payment for the policy limits, plus additional living expenses, plus contents. I then asked her about the ring. She told me her ex-husband was a professional baseball player and had bought it for her, confirming that it was also in the fire. "Do you have any idea where?" I asked. "I put all of my jewelry in a soap dish every night before I go to bed," she replied.

I told her to stay where she was, and I'd be right back.

The bathroom was easy to find because of the scorched plumbing. I picked up a short piece of charred two-by-four and started stirring through the remains of the sink and vanity. Soon, I saw a melted piece of plastic. I picked it up and there, melted into the plastic, was the ring, with that big rock looking at me. I took it to her and asked if it was her ring. She dropped the toddler as she started crying and gave me a big hug.

When I arrived back at the BCO, I told them we would pay policy limits on all the coverages, including the ring, which was indeed in the fire. I added that they shouldn't judge a customer until they had done a thorough investigation.

She called me a few days later with the news that her jeweler would be able to repair the ring for $1,600, which I thought was a bargain.

Chapter 24

Papa Bear

In the spring of 2007, I was transferred to Jacksonville, Florida, to review claims. While I didn't really care about this job, the pay was based on a day rate, so you know how much money you'll make. I gathered up my tools of the trade and moved into my own cubical, right next to Wade Evans.

Wade was a big, loud, burly guy who I thought was obnoxious and crude, which he was. I was amazed that Human Resources hadn't already locked him out of the building for some of the comments he made. After a week or so, I confronted Wade and told him the reason they put me next to him was because I was the only guy that could put up with his nonsense.

The good thing about Wade was that he didn't pick on any particular person because of their ethnicity, gender, or sexual orientation. He just picked on everyone. I have Parkinson's, so my nickname was, of course, "Shakey." Wade was also a Vietnam helicopter pilot, so after living in the hell of that small country, he had earned respect. Wade also knew policy inside out. Now, I'm also pretty good at policy interpretation. We would often bounce different scenarios off each other until we agreed on an answer. It wasn't long until we were known throughout the office, by rookies and seasoned adjusters, as the go-to guys for policy issues. Both Wade and I were happy to help anyone who asked for it.

One day, he came to my cubical and quietly asked me to give him my opinion on something. "Okay, Papa Bear, what have you got?" I asked. "Read this and tell me what you think," he said.

At that time, Citizens was not paying for contents that were outside, such as patio furniture and barbeque grills. We were only paying for them if they were in a fully-enclosed structure and had been since at least 2004. I looked up the word "enclosed" and read an example, "The mountains enclose the valley."

"Oh crap!" I exclaimed. "We have been interpreting the policy incorrectly for years."

"I agree," Wade said. "What's our next move?"

Our next move was to go to our manager, who read it twice, as I had, until the magnitude of our discovery slowly sank in. Her draw jaw dropped, and her eyes got bigger. "What are you going to do?" she asked.

"The only thing we can do," we replied. "We are going to start paying for contents in any yard that's fenced in."

She advised that we should talk to the designated go-to guy about policy issues. We walked around the building and found him, yeah you guessed it, near the coffee machine and showed him what the policy said.

"So, what?" he responded, unfazed.

"So, what?" I said, taken aback. "We have been denying damaged contents unless they are in a fully-covered building for years. The policy states it must be an enclosed structure, which is what a fence is."

I continued, "At this time, we can honestly say that it was just an unintentional misinterpretation of the policy. Now, since we know the truth, it becomes bad faith if we don't start allowing coverage for items that we know our policy covers and are now subject to a possible class action lawsuit."

We explained that, as per the policy, a fence is a structure. Further, if it surrounds the yard, it is an enclosed structure.

He remarked, "That's above my pay grade. I'm not going to touch this."

I don't know who talked to who, or exactly what was said. All I know is, about two hours later, you guessed it, the liaison for the company I was working for escorted me from the building. Three days after that, he did the same with Wade. Wade and I can't prove it, but we were fired for pointing out a flaw in the policy. However, even if it cost us our jobs, it was the right thing to do.

Citizens Insurance is owned by the state of Florida. To change the verbiage of a policy takes a vote by the Florida Legislature.

I found out later that the wording had been changed by the next storm season to read, "Contents must be inside a fully enclosed structure."

Rest in Peace Wade Evans

Cowboy Pirate

My wife and I were working claims all over the Miami and Ft. Lauderdale area, and we were killing it. I would take measurements and call them out in Xactimate codes, and she would write them down in the order I called out. This made it a breeze to enter in the computer for a finished estimate. My nephew, Drew Jackson, was also there doing the ladder work and climbing roofs with Jeff Wilson. They would often assist in measuring areas as I instructed them. We were staying in an RV park in Ft. Lauderdale, which might have been the noisiest RV park in America. It was located along the final flight path for the Ft. Lauderdale International Airport. If that wasn't enough, there was also a commuter train and a freeway between my RV and the runway. To say noise was constant would be an understatement.

During our stay there, I noticed a cute Latino lady visiting nearly every RV in the park. I soon found out she was married to an adjuster who never seemed to be away from his computer. Don't get me wrong, I worked hard, but I can only stay hooked up to a computer writing estimates for so long before I need to take a break.

When I managed to break free, I would walk or ride my bike around the park for fifteen minutes and then go back to my RV and work. Any time I was out, I would see this guy and wave at him. He seldom waved back and found out his name was Rick Bruenner.

He must really be a jerk, I'd think to myself. One day, I ran into him at the park office, and we chatted for a few minutes. After a few rounds of small talk, I discovered he was relatively new to the business.

However, he was one of the most focused guys I'd ever met. We formed a friendship that has lasted more than sixteen years, and I assume will last many more.

The RV park had a marina and on one New Year's Eve, we were sitting under my awning drinking rum and coke and smoking hand-rolled Cuban cigars.

While watching a giant iguana sun himself, I said out loud, "Ya know, I've never roped an iguana."

Rick replied, "You can't rope an iguana."

What Rick didn't know was that I came from a rodeo background and always carried a kid's rope to play with when I got bored. Before he knew it, I had grabbed my Rope, and two swings later, I had the four-foot long, pissed-off lizard at the end of my rope.

Rick spilled his rum and dropped his cigar, as he was laughing his ass off. That's how you make lifelong friends.

Neither Rick nor I were happy with the location of our RV park. And we certainly were not happy with the manager who had learned all her public relations skills from a Gestapo captain. On January 1, Rick moved to an RV park that my nephew, Drew, had found for us in Key Largo. It was quiet, as it only had about ten spots and a marina.

I had almost all my inspections completed but had mountains of paperwork to do. My advice to new adjusters is not to get behind with your paperwork, but commercial claims are different. You can't scope a condominium with a hundred units in one day. Then, say you have one-hundred different condominiums, they all want to see your smiling face, so it becomes a major juggling act.

I moved to Key Largo on February 1st. On February 3rd, I had a twenty-one-foot boat in the RV marina. Evon said, "I can't believe you bought a boat." I replied, "I can't believe you thought I'd be in the Florida Keys without one."

This was the best gig I had ever had. I bought a red Radio Flyer wagon at Target and mounted rod holders on each side. The wagon easily held my small ice chest and tackle box. I could ride my bicycle to the bait shop a half mile away and by the time I got there I'd know if I wanted to fish the everglades or the open ocean which was separated by this thin strip of land, which they called Key Largo. If Evon woke up and looked out the window and find my wagon wasn't there, she'd know I was fishing. I'd normally fish for an hour or so, and then return to the RV and do paper work until the need for a nap overcame my need to sit behind my computer. Then, I'd retire to my hammock, which was hanging between two palm trees.

This work schedule lasted from February to April that year, until I finally wrapped up my end of that storm and had my little run in with the file examiner we met in the previous chapter.

So, here I was, recently unemployed and heading back to Key Largo to clear my head and catch a few fish. Rick and I fished Friday and Saturday, and unfortunately, Rick had to run into Miami to do a couple of inspections, so I decided to fish on Sunday by myself. I had watched the Weather Channel late into the previous night, and their forecast called for a storm to pass through around 11 a.m.

I woke up later than I had planned, possibly due to the multiple rum and cokes I'd had the night before. I thought I would not fish as long as I had planned so I could get back before the squall arrived. On the way out to one of my favorite reefs, a beautiful sail fish exploded out of the water about thirty yards in front of me. I rigged up two poles and started trolling in an attempt to catch this beauty.

Later, I noticed the wind picking up and a very dark cloud in the north. I didn't take time to reel in my bait. I just cut the lines and turned into the wind as I powered up my 115 horsepower Yamaha Outboard for the five-mile run back to Key Largo. The wind-driven waves were coming over the bow and soaking me each time. I hid behind the console whenever I saw one coming, and needless to say, I wasn't making much headway. The vent tube for the fuel tank was on the side of the boat and with all of the dunkings my little boat was taking on water. Eventually, water got into the fuel line, and the engine died.

Well, this ain't good, I thought to myself.

At that moment, I made a wise decision. I put my pride aside and called 911, which put me in contact with the

Coast Guard. I told the nice guy on the phone about my situation and gave him my GPS coordinates. He told me he would get a Coast Guard boat on its way; but if it was okay with me, he would send a commercial tow boat instead, because they could get to me sooner. I told him sooner sounded great, and he said someone should arrive within thirty-five minutes.

I have this gift, or maybe it's a curse, that I can fall asleep anywhere. I had around thirty minutes before rescue would arrive, so I laid my head on the console and soon I was asleep. After about ten or fifteen minutes, the Coast Guard fellow called me back just to check on my situation. That's when I realized my boat's bilge pump could not keep up with the amount of water coming over the bow and sides of the boat.

"Uh, I have a problem," I stammered. "The boat is taking on massive amounts of water and is rolling over as we speak. Hope to see you soon!"

Immediately after saying that, I was in the water and all my life jackets were in a bag, which was stored on the bottom of the T-Top above my head. Due to (I hope my mother doesn't read this) stupidity or arrogance, or an equal amount of both, I didn't have on life jacket.

So here I am, five miles off the Florida coast, hanging onto a capsized boat with four life jackets about six feet below me underwater. Then, like a beacon from Heaven, my throw cushion popped up and floated past me. I had no idea how long the capsized boat would float, but I knew the cushion would float forever. So, weighing my options, I swam to the cushion. I hugged it like a newborn hugged their mother.

Another thing I had in my favor was that I was a very good swimmer and I decided I would try for thirty seconds to get back to the boat. So, I swam towards the boat as hard as I could. When I swam for what I thought was thirty seconds, I stopped and looked around. Swimming against the high wind and with the six-foot waves crashing all around, my progress was just a meager two or three feet.

I abandoned my plan and went to plan B, which was to hang onto the yellow throw cushion and wait for the Coast Guard to pluck me out of the water. The good news was it was only around noon, which gave them six or seven hours to look for me, plus I had given them my GPS co-ordinates. That would let them drive within inches of where I was when the boat capsized. However, I didn't take into consideration how far the boat would be blown away those coordinates. I was a good two or three-hundred yards away from my wet entry when the rescue boat arrived. They were circling my last known location, searching for me. The six-foot seas were not helping any. It was impossible for them to see me when I was between waves. Every time I rode a wave to its crest, I would raise the cushion above my head. Finally, my rescuers pointed their boat towards me and powered up.

Yippee, yi, yi, yeah! I said to myself. *They see me!* They eased up to me and one of crew members yelled, "Are you Mr. Phillips, or Phelps, or anything like that?" Now, my name is fairly easy to pronounce. It's one syllable and has no "L's."

It was all I could do not to answer, "How many dumbasses are you looking for? Are there more than me out here? You know, I passed a guy a little while ago. I think that might be his name." But I followed one of my other better judgment rules: don't be a smart ass to your rescue boat while you're still in the water.

"Yep. That's me" I responded instead.

He helped onto his boat and sheepishly asked, "That was kind of a stupid question, wasn't it?"

I answered, "Man, I would have been anyone you wanted to be. I'd be Elvis, Santa, Jimmy Hoffa, whoever – just let me on your boat."

On the way back to Key Largo, I asked the captain if I could use his cell phone to call my wife.

She answered, "What's up?"

"I sunk my boat," I said.

"No, really, what's up?" she asked again.

"I sunk my boat," I repeated.

Still, not totally believing me, she asked, "Whose phone are you calling from?"

I told her, "Captain Ron's. Mine's wet."

Realizing I might be serious, she asked, "You really did sink your boat, didn't you?"

"I told you I sunk it," I answered.

"Where's Rick?" she asked.

I told her, "He had to work today."

"And you went fishing by yourself?!" She exclaimed.

"Yep," I said quietly.

"There's supposed to be a storm today," she continued.

"There was," I confirmed.

"I don't know what to say," she replied.

"You love me? You're glad I survived?" I posed. I knew she was really pissed off when she hung up on me.

When I made it back to Rick's RV, he asked, "Hey man, where's your boat?"

Confused, he asked, "What do you mean, 'Out there?'"

After repeating the conversation I'd had with my wife, he then said, "I'm going to get you a t-shirt that says, "I need adult supervision.

The Race is On

There's an old saying that goes, "He or she who contacts the agent first wins." This means, when an adjuster really upsets a customer and leaves the property, the one who contacts the agent first and explains their side of the story wins. There's nothing an agent hates more than getting blindsided by a pissed-off client without knowing any details. If you've upset their customer, drive around the block, call the agent, and explain your side of the story.

Nut House

I once worked for an independent firm out of Mobile, Alabama, after Hurricane Katrina. A friend of mine had been hired by them to be the Catastrophe Director and recruited me to be the Assistant Catastrophe Director. This company was backed by a lawyer with deep pockets who wasn't afraid to spend money. His CEO was a cocky, overrated man who didn't know anything about adjusting or the business. He often boasted that they were not adjusters trying to get into the insurance business, but businessmen trying to get into the insurance business.

Robert's idea of fixing a problem was to throw technology at it. One day, we were in a high-level meeting, and he was introducing some new whiz-bang idea on how to reinvent the wheel. I offered a simpler solution.

"Kenny, why would you want to do it that way?" he asked.

I said, "Because it works, and it has for a long time. You're trying to reinvent the wheel, and you don't have a clue what one looks like."

After the meeting, the owner and one of his mentors pulled me into a tiny office and asked, "What the hell was that all about?"

A little defensively, I said, "Well, sir, you wanted to build a bus. So, you built one. And it is a really nice bus. All leather seats with WiFi at every seat and a little work station, The bus is amazing, except it doesn't have a steering wheel. You hired Jimmy and me to steer your shiny new bus, but your CEO won't listen to us. I'm afraid your bus is going to run off the road and my concern is that I'm not sure the airbags will deploy in time to save my ass."

He nodded his head as if he understood and thanked me for my honesty.

I had recruited a friend of mine, who I called T-bird to do file review and basically manage the office. She was a wiz with policy and reviewing files, plus she was funny and smart. During our tenure, a couple of guys sold their alleged talents and knowledge to the owner and were starting to tell Jimmy and me how to manage our adjusters, which Jimmy and I didn't care for. I decided those two guys had just been in sales without any experience in catastrophe adjusting.

As you may have guessed, most of our claims were in New Orleans, and adjusters were spending much of their time looking for gas or sitting in line to buy a few gallons of gas. Adjuster morale was close to zero, and a few of them had left for cleanup duty in Florida. I was driving to the office one day, when I saw a vacant gas station for rent. I called the number in the window and explained to the gentleman I was interested in renting his station for a month. He said he would lease it to me, and we agreed on a reasonable price. I then called a couple of friends back home who were in the wholesale gasoline business to see if they could bring me a load of 5,000 gallons.

They both assured me there would be no problem and asked when I wanted it. I thought it was one of the better ideas I'd had in a long time. We would hire a college kid to work there, and we'd sell gas to adjusters only for enough to pay for our expenses. The adjusters would be thrilled to be able to work claims instead of waiting in line for gasoline. I met Robert in the hall and told him my idea.

He laughed and said, "What are you trying to do, put us in the convenience store business?" He then turned his back to me and walked off, still chuckling. That's when I realized I wouldn't be here much longer.

My daughter was getting married soon, and I left to be at her wedding. The day before I left, I was called into the office of one of the mentors, and he told me they were going to send me to Houston to straighten of a mess caused by the team lead they had sent there to manage.

He then told me if I couldn't repair the damage, I most likely would not have a job when I returned to Mobile. I took that as a threat, and if you know me, you know I don't do well when threatened.

Well, I went to the wedding and danced with the beautiful bride, then went to Houston, straightened out the mess there, and returned to Mobile to a very cool atmosphere. T-bird and I shared an office. I wasn't included in inter-office memos, emails, or meetings. When I'd walk in a room, things would get so quiet you'd think I was carrying a disease.

I'd had enough of the silent treatment and went to the office at 6 a.m. one morning. I opened T-bird's computer and read her emails and didn't find anything flattering about me. It was clear that it was time to pull the plug. T-bird came in about 7:30 and found me drinking a cup of coffee and eating a donut. She sat at her desk and when she found her computer running, she exploded.

"What have you been doing in my computer?" she fumed.

"Catching up on emails," I replied. "Some of them are pretty interesting. Have you read them?"

She stormed out of the room and made a beeline to Robert's office. I knew I would get a call soon, so I finished my donut and coffee and waited. Sure enough, my phone rang about ten minutes later.

"Kenny, would you come to my office?" Robert said on the other line.

"On my way boss," I cheerily remarked.

I sat across from him. His huge wooden desk wasn't nearly as large as his ego.

He started by saying, "We knew we were going to have to relocate you, because T-bird did a great job while you were gone. This is an entirely different situation, however."

I replied, "Robert, don't you think if I was smart enough to open her computer, I'd be smart enough to get out of it without her knowing?"

His facial expression went blank. "You knew she'd find out?" he asked, trying to understand what I was getting at.

"Why, yes," I retorted.

He knew he'd been busted and asked, "What will it take to get you to leave quietly?"

So, we negotiated an amount agreeable to both of us, I shook his hand and left. On my way out he said, "Kenny, I've never met anyone quite like you."

"And if you're lucky, you never will," I replied. As I was packing my stuff, one of the mentors came to me and told me many of the adjusters were not paying policy limits on obvious total losses on the beaches, which was drastically affecting the fee we charged the carrier. I told him that they were not all caused by the wind, and we would not be able to determine that without an engineer's report. He demanded that I tell the adjusters to pay policy limits on the total loss claims.

I pulled up a picture on my computer, which showed an obvious line of debris, in which every structure on the ocean side was leveled. On the mainland side, many of the structures were damaged, but not totaled. Again, he told me to instruct the adjusters to pay for them.

I told him to write me a memo stating he ordered me to have the adjusters to pay for the structures on the ocean side of the debris line. He refused. I told him he refused because he knew I was right, and I also told him that he was a jerk.

Oh, in case you're wondering where I got the title for this story – the building we worked out of was called the Planter's Building.

Florida Gold Rush

The year 2004 was the craziest year I'd ever seen. In a normal year there might be six or seven named storms with only two or three that threatened the mainland from the Outer Banks to the Texas Gulf Coast. We witnessed some truly amazing events, which started on August thirteenth, when Hurricane Charlie came ashore just west of Fort Meyers with sustained winds of 150 mph.

Let me get up on my stump for a little bit. I live in Oklahoma. We've had our fair share of bad weather, including tornados, windstorms and hailstorms. However, the local weathermen and weatherwomen, when forecasting impending storms, would always say, "Beware of possible hurricane-force winds."

What? Hurricane-force winds? While it's true that the leading edge of a storm may have winds of 75 mph or more, they rarely last more than five or ten minutes. I've been in several hurricanes, and those have sustained winds that last ten to twelve hours. That is a huge difference. My local guy is trying to make our ten-minute exposure to 75 mph wind as dramatic as a ten-hour pounding by 100-150 mph winds. On September Fifth, Hurricane Frances made landfall as a meager category-two on the East Coast.

On September sixteenth, Hurricane Ivan made landfall with 120 mile per hour winds near Gulf Shores, Alabama.

Pepcon Explosion

On May 7, 1988, I was finishing a small hailstorm in Duncan, Oklahoma, when my phone rang. It was Pat Wardlaw, the owner of Wardlaw Claims Service, and he sounded pretty excited.

"Kenny! How soon can you get here? They keep saying this is going to be a major event, and I need you out here as soon as you can."

I told him I was wrapping this storm and could be there in two days.

"Ok, that's great. Get here as soon as you can." Pat replied.

"No problem," I said. "I have one question. Where are you?"

He answered, "Las Vegas."

"What happened there, a windstorm?" I questioned.

"No dammit. Haven't you seen the news? A plant that makes rocket fuel blew up and leveled the plant."

Two days later I pulled into the motel parking lot and checked into my room. I still didn't believe the amount of destruction I was going to find. The main explosion and subsequent explosions killed two people, injured 372 others and caused an estimate of one-hundred million dollars.

The plant was in a valley between Henderson and Las Vegas. The first house I inspected was at the edge of the plateau overlooking the plant about ¾ of a mile away and my initial estimate was $87,000.00.

Many houses had every window that faced the plant was blown out with shards of glass imbedded in the opposite wall. Every garage door for blocks that faced the plant was blown in. The attic access panels were blown out, ruining the carpet and clothes with insulation that covered everything.

Another thing that made this event unusual was it was okay with the carrier to accept gratuities from our customers. Their logic was as long as they were coupons for buffets for meals or shows and the homeowner did not pay for them it was okay to accept them. Las Vegas lives on buffets and casinos. Adjusters had coupons on their motel desks, and we traded them like baseball cards. I'll trade you three Stardust Buffets for two Caesars steaks. It was crazy.

About three years after I left Vegas I received a phone call from Matt Fatheree, one of the partners with Wardlaw saying I had been subpoenaed to be dispositioned concerning my handling my files at the Pepcon event. He said that the carriers co-insures say you overpaid every claim knowing that subrogation would most likely be involved.

Subrogation is when the insurance may pay their policyholder for their damages, then they'd go after the party responsible for the damages and collect from them. Sure enough, within a week I was contacted by the law firm, Wee, Cheetum, and Howe and agreed to meet them at the Holiday Inn in my hometown of Ardmore and to be prepared to stay there all day.

On the appointed day I met with two attorneys representing the bad guys, and one really big guy from Utah to keep me in line.

One of the bad cop lawyer's I knew I wouldn't like. She was snappy with her questions and couldn't hide her disdain for me behind those designer glasses. She was obviously a corporation ladder climber and was counting the seconds before she would be through with this assignment. The other bad cop was a younger guy who had taken the opportunity to visit a couple of his old fraternity brothers, enjoying the Dallas night life. He was so hungover that he could barely lift his head from the table.

The guy sent to protect me was, like I'd said earlier, a big guy. He didn't know in beginning the how hard it was going to be keeping the "she-devil" and me from ripping each others tonsils out. The interrogation drug slowly on, and I felt like a prisoner of war who was having bamboo shoots forced under my fingernails. It was agony. We ordered a couple of pizza's for lunch, allowing us to slow down the interrogation. The she devil had every claim I had worked in a couple of boxes and notes on all of them noting my transgressions. I spoke only when questioned.

When our time in purgatory was almost up she and the other two were franticly looking for a certain file while I twiddled my thumbs watching them. She noticed I was searching for the file and asked me why I wasn't looking for the mystery file.

"I found it." I responded.

"Why didn't you tell me?" She asked. I noticed the veins in her neck looking like they were about to burst.

"Because you didn't say please." I said, the veins nearing the bursting pressure.

That was the last bit of insubordination she could stand and called the meeting over. My representative went outside to smoke, and I followed him. I asked him if we were finished, and he said yes.

"You mean I can talk to her and it is off the record?"

"Yes." he cautiously replied." What are you going to say?"

"I'm just going to tell her goodbye."

"Why do I feel like I need to go with you?" He asked.

"Because you may enjoy it." I said.

I walked up to her and while I shook her hand I said, "You beat me up like I've never been beat up before. And I don't like you and you don't like me, and that's okay because if there is a God in Heaven, we will never see each other again."

"However, there is something I think you should know." I continued.

"And that is?" she questioned.

"You have a really nice ass!"

My guy grabbed my arm and was dragging me toward the door. "You crazy SOB. You can't say that to her."

"C'mon man, just look at it, it's perfect, and those legs, they should be in a museum."

She was shaking visibly and looked like the buttons had all been pressed to launch one of the Saturn rockets, but had forgot to pull the safety pin which kept it from leaving the launch pad.

Daggers were flying from her eyes and were bouncing off my body like Styrofoam darts from my son's toy gun.

He said, "She'll sue you, man."

I looked her in her bloodshot eyes and said, "Sue me? For a compliment in my hometown. Sue me Baby, sue me." I then blew her a kiss and walked out the door.

About Kenny Phipps

Born and raised on a ranch near the southern Oklahoma village of Woodford, Kenny grew up around working cowboys. The smell of horse sweat and saddle soap was burned into his mind at an early age.

By the early spring 1979, Kenny was an ex-rodeo cowboy and a two-time junior college dropout who had no idea where the future would lead him. A family friend, Jim Wright, approached Kenny and asked him what he was going to do with his life. Kenny answered, "I don't know, but I have a beautiful young blonde wife I need to support. I need to find something more lucrative than working at the tire factory, building tires." Jim remarked, "Boy, come with me, and I'll show you how to make money." Jim's offer gave Kenny a thirty-year career as an independent claims adjuster.

What can an Oklahoma cowboy, who spent his life on the road re-establishing damaged lives and homes as an insurance adjuster, tell us about life as well as our own lives? A good amount!

Kenny was diagnosed with Parkinson's disease in 1999, and he has considered it a nuisance. He honestly believes the disease has been a blessing, because he began to view the meaning of life differently and became more committed to his family and friends. He started writing poetry in March 2004. You can read about his observations and escapades in his four books.

Kenny has written these cowboy-related books: *Rhymes & Times of a Parrothead Cowboy, Dooley's Legacy, and Just a Cowboy – More Rhymes & Times.* Kenny admits his poetry is not classic, but rather modern cowboy poetry. His short stories will make you laugh and shed a tear.

Kenny's still observing and creating new escapades, and maybe someday we'll read about them.

ORDER COPIES OF THIS BOOK NOW!

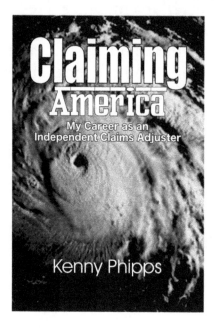

NO. OF COPIES_____ @ $16.95 each_____ x no. of copies

SUBTOTAL _____

Add 4.5% sales tax (Okla. residents only) _____
Postage and handling for 1st book - $4.25 _____
P & H for each additional book - $1.00 _____

TOTAL _____

ORDERED BY_____

STREET/APT NO._____

CITY/STATE/ZIP_____

PHONE (_____)_____

Your email address:_____
We would like to send you product updates by email.

MAKE YOUR CHECK OR MONEY ORDER TO: Kenny Phipps

PLEASE MAIL THIS ORDER FORM WITH YOUR PAYMENT TO:

Kenny Phipps, 2749 Edgewood Rd., Ardmore, OK 73401
Please allow 2 weeks for delivery. Prices are subject to change without notice.

ORDER COPIES OF THIS BOOK NOW!

NO. OF COPIES_____ @ $14.⁹⁵ each_____x no. of copies

SUBTOTAL _____

Add 4.5% sales tax (Okla. residents only) _____

Postage and handling for 1st book - $4.²⁵ _____

P & H for each additional book - $1.⁰⁰ _____

TOTAL _____

ORDERED BY_____

STREET/APT NO._____

CITY/STATE/ZIP_____

PHONE (_____)_____

Your email address:_____
We would like to send you product updates by email.

MAKE YOUR CHECK OR MONEY ORDER TO: Kenny Phipps

PLEASE MAIL THIS ORDER FORM WITH YOUR PAYMENT TO:

Kenny Phipps, 2749 Edgewood Rd., Ardmore, OK 73401

Please allow 2 weeks for delivery. Prices are subject to change without notice.

Visit our Website:
kennyphippscowboypoet.com

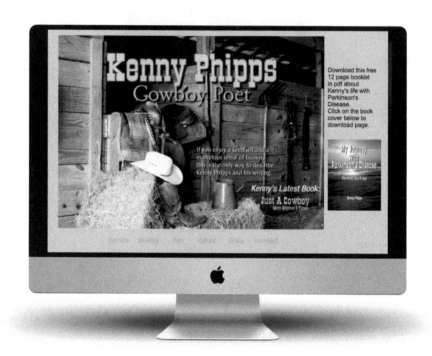

Everyone has a story to tell.

Have you written a book?

InCahoots Literary
could be your
PUBLISHER

We take your manuscript, put it in book form and place your new book in the marketplace. We can also develop your promotional and marketing strategies. We love authors who will promote and sell their books in every possible way.

For more information, visit our Web site:
www.incahootsliterary.com

You can view our latest book releases and order our published books.

CPSIA information can be obtained
at www.ICGtesting.com
Printed in the USA
BVHW092035061122
650917BV00005B/91